MW00512605

THE ESSENTIAL BOOK FOR MAKING ARTISAN CHEESE AT HOME

100 EASY AND TASTY TECHNIQUES AND RECIPES

GRAYSON SHAW

All rights reserved.

Disclaimer

The information contained in this eBook is meant to serve as a comprehensive collection of strategies that the author of this eBook has done research about. Summaries, strategies, tips and tricks are only recommendation by the author, and reading this eBook will not guarantee that one's results will exactly mirror the author's results. The author of the eBook has made all reasonable effort to provide current and accurate information for the readers of the eBook. The author and its associates will not be held liable for any unintentional error or omissions that may be found. The material in the eBook may include information by third parties. Third party materials comprise of opinions expressed by their owners. As such, the author of the eBook does not assume responsibility or liability for any third party material or opinions. Whether because of the progression of the internet, or the unforeseen changes in company policy and editorial submission guidelines, what is stated as fact at the time of this writing may become outdated or inapplicable later.

The eBook is copyright © 2022 with all rights reserved. It is illegal to redistribute, copy, or create derivative work from this eBook whole or in part. No parts of this report may be reproduced or retransmitted in any reproduced or retransmitted in any forms whatsoever without the writing expressed and signed permission from the author.

TABLE OF CONTENTS

COATED AND RUBBED CHEESES...............................283

BLOOMY-RIND AND SURFACE-RIPENED CHEESES 312

INTRODUCTION

Cheese is a preserved form of milk made by the coagulation, draining or pressing, and salting of the milk proteins and fats. It is popular for its versatility, longevity, portability, and nutritional value. Cheese is a stable food with a longer shelf life than milk, and it is an affordable food for any budget. There are numerous styles, shapes, tastes, and textures of cheese, all developed in different regions, climates, and cultures of the world.

Cheese is a very popular food that can be found on the shelves of any grocery store, though the cheese found in the dairy section is often a highly processed food containing additives and preservatives.

In contrast, your homemade cheese can be free of all of the colorings and chemical stabilizers used to make cheese more attractive and stable for store shelves. Your homemade cheese will be better-tasting, more alive, and more versatile than any commercially processed cheese.

While you may encounter challenges when you try something new, as a whole, cheese making is a very rewarding and simple process. The most basic cheeses require only a few ingredients and tools. Basic cheese making is surprisingly forgiving, and most cheese making failures are still edible. So enjoy whatever cheese you create and make adjustments on the next attempt.

Making your own cheese will not only be healthier and more nourishing to your family, but the world of cheese making is so wide and diverse, you may find yourself with a new and very addicting hobby!

VEGAN CHEESE

1.   Cashew cheddar

Ingredients

- 1 cup raw cashews
- 1 cup filtered water
- 1 teaspoon Himalayan salt
- $\frac{1}{4}$ cup modified tapioca starch
- Beta-carotene squeezed from 2 gel caps
- **1/4** cup refined coconut oil, plus more for greasing the pan
- 1$\frac{1}{2}$ teaspoons agar-agar powder
- Place the cashews in filtered water in a small bowl. Cover and refrigerate overnight.

Directions

a) Drain the cashews. In the pitcher of a Blender, place the cashews, water, modified tapioca starch, beta-carotene, coconut oil, and agar-agar powder.

b) Blend on high speed until smooth.

c) Oil a 4.5 x 1-inch round spring form pan with coconut oil.

d) Transfer the cashew mixture to a saucepan and heat on medium-low, stirring continuously, until it becomes thick and cheese-like in consistency. (You can use a thermometer and heat the mixture to about 145 degrees F. See here for tips on this technique.)

e) At this stage, you can spread this warm, thick cheese onto toasted bread for a delicious sandwich. or you can fold the cheese into the prepared mold .and set it aside to cool.

f) Refrigerate the cheese overnight to set up.

g) Run a knife around the inside edge of the mold. Release the buckle on the spring form pan and, using the flat edge of a large knife, release the cheese from the bottom metal round.

h) Transfer to a cutting board. Using a sharp knife, slice the cheese and serve

2.   Smoked Gouda

Ingredients

- 1/4 cup raw cashews
- 1/4 cup raw almonds
- 1/4 cup refined coconut oil, plus more for greasing
- 1 cup filtered water
- 1/4 cup modified tapioca starch
- 1 drop beta-carotene, squeezed out of the gel cap
- 1 teaspoon Himalayan salt
- $2\frac{1}{2}$ tablespoons agar-agar flakes
- 1 teaspoon liquid smoke

Directions

a) Place the cashews in filtered water in a small bowl. Cover and refrigerate overnight. Place the almonds in filtered water in a small bowl. Cover and refrigerate overnight.

b) Lightly oil a 4-inch spring form pan with coconut oil.

c) Drain the cashews.

d) Bring 4 cups of water to a boil in a medium saucepan over medium-high heat. Add the almonds and blanch them for 1 minute. Drain the almonds in a colander and remove the skins with your fingers (you can compost the skins).

e) In the pitcher of a Blender, place the cashews, almonds, water, the modified tapioca starch, beta-carotene, coconut oil, salt, and agar-agar.

f) Blend on high speed for 1 minute or until smooth.

g) Transfer the mixture to a saucepan and heat over medium-low heat, stirring continuously, until it becomes thick and cheese-like in consistency. (You can use a thermometer and heat the mixture to about 145 degrees F. See here for tips on this technique.)

h) Add in the liquid smoke and mix with a rubber spatula to incorporate well.

i) Pour the cheese into the prepared spring form pan. Smooth the cheese with the back of a spoon coated with coconut oil. Let the mixture cool, then cover it with a parchment paper round cut to the size of the cheese mold. Transfer the cheese to the fridge overnight to set up.

Run a sharp knife around the inside edge of the pan. Release the buckle and remove the ring of the mold. Using the flat edge of a large knife, separate the cheese from the bottom metal round and transfer to a cutting board. With a very sharp knife, slice the cheese and serve

3.   Mozzarella balls in brine

Ingredients

- 1 cup raw cashews
- 1 cup raw almonds

Brine

- 12 cups filtered water
- 2 tablespoons to $\frac{1}{4}$ cup Himalayan pink salt
- 1 cup filtered water
- 1/4 cup modified tapioca starch
- 1/4 cup refined coconut oil
- 1 teaspoon Himalayan salt
- $2\frac{1}{2}$ tablespoons agar-agar flakes or $1\frac{1}{2}$ teaspoons agar-agar powder

Directions

a) Place the cashews in filtered water in a small bowl. Cover and refrigerate overnight.

b) Rinse the almonds well. Place them in water in a small bowl. Cover and refrigerate overnight.

c) Prepare a brine solution by bringing the water to a boil in a large saucepan over high heat and adding the salt until it dissolves.

d) Transfer the brine to a ceramic bowl and place in the freezer.

e) Bring 4 cups water to a boil in a medium saucepan over medium-high heat. Add the almonds and blanch them for 1 minute. Drain the almonds in a colander and remove the skins with your fingers (you can compost the skins).

f) Drain the cashews. In the bowl of a Blender, place the cashews, almonds, water, modified tapioca starch, coconut oil, salt, and agar-agar.

g) Blend on high speed for 1 minute or until smooth.

h) Transfer the mixture to a saucepan and, stirring continuously, heat over medium-low heat until it becomes thick and cheese-like in consistency. (You can use a thermometer and heat the mixture to about 145 degrees F. See here for tips on this technique.)

i) Scoop the warm cheese from the saucepan with an ice cream scooper and drop it into the brine.

j) Add 1 cup of ice to the cheese in brine mixture. Cover and transfer to the fridge and refrigerate overnight.

4.   Cashew-almond mozzarella

Ingredients

- 1 cup raw cashews
- 1 cup almonds
- 1 teaspoon apple cider vinegar
- 1 teaspoon Celtic sea salt
- One 15-ounce can coconut milk
- 1/4 cup refined coconut oil
- 1 cup filtered water
- $\frac{1}{2}$ cup agar-agar flakes

Directions

a) Place the cashews in filtered water in a small bowl. Cover and refrigerate overnight.

b) Rinse the almonds well. Place them in water in a small bowl. Cover and refrigerate overnight.

c) Line two 6-inch rectangular nonstick molds with plastic wrap, leaving enough excess plastic wrap hanging over the sides to wrap the mixture once it's cooled.

d) Bring 4 cups of water to a boil in a medium saucepan over medium-high heat. Add the almonds and blanch them for 1 minute. Drain the almonds in a colander and remove the skins with your fingers (you can compost the skins). Drain the cashews. In the bowl of a food processor, place the almonds and cashews and pulse until they are mealy in texture. Add the vinegar and salt. Pulse again a few times to combine.

e) In a small saucepan over medium heat, combine the coconut milk, coconut oil, and water. When the mixture is warmed through, add the agar-agar flakes and stir constantly until the agar-agar is dissolved.

f) With the motor running, pour the mixture into the food processor tube and blend until the mixture is creamy. Stop the motor, remove the lid, and scrape down the sides. Process again to make sure the mixture gets incorporated well. This can also be done in the Blender for a smoother texture.

g) Pour the mixture into the prepared molds and let cool on the counter. After the cheese has cooled, cover it with the excess plastic wrap and refrigerate for 24 hours or until firm.

h) Turn the cheese out of the molds and slice. Use as a pizza topping or inside a tomato basil panini!

5.   Vegan Provolone

Ingredients

- 1 cup raw cashews
- 1 cup filtered water
- 1/4 cup refined coconut oil, plus more for greasing the pan
- 1/4 cup modified tapioca starch
- 2 drops beta-carotene, squeezed out of the gel cap
- 1 teaspoon white truffle oil
- 1 teaspoon Himalayan salt
- $1\frac{1}{2}$ teaspoons agar-agar powder or $2\frac{1}{2}$ tablespoons agar-agar flakes

Directions

a) Place the cashews in filtered water in a small bowl. Cover and refrigerate overnight.

b) Lightly oil a 4.5 x 1.5-inch spring form pan with coconut oil.

c) Drain the cashews. In the pitcher of a Blender, place the cashews, water, modified tapioca starch, beta-carotene, coconut oil, truffle oil, salt, and agar-agar. Blend on high speed for 1 minute or until smooth.

d) Transfer the mixture to a small saucepan over medium-low heat and stir continuously until it becomes thick and cheese-like in consistency.

e) Pour the cheese into the prepared spring form pan. Let it cool. Cover with a parchment round cut to the size of the mold, then transfer to the fridge overnight to set up

f) Turn the cheese out of the mold and place on a serving plate. Using a very sharp knife, slice it and eat it with Kale Chip

6.   Macadamia nut herbed goat cheese

Ingredients

- 2 cups raw macadamia nuts
- 1 capsule acidophilus (3-billion-active-culture strain)
- 1 teaspoon plus $\frac{1}{8}$ teaspoon Celtic sea salt
- 1/4 cup coconut milk
- 2 teaspoons refined coconut oil
- 1 teaspoon Himalayan salt
- 2 tablespoons Greek spices or za'atar (a blend of thyme, oregano, and marjoram)

Directions

a) In the pitcher of a Blender, place the macadamia nuts, acidophilus, $\frac{1}{2}$ teaspoon Celtic sea salt, coconut milk, coconut oil, and the Himalayan salt. Blend on medium speed, using the plunger to evenly distribute the mixture.

b) Transfer the mixture to the center of an 8-inch piece of cheesecloth. Gather the edges together and tie off your bundle with string. Place the cheese bundle in the dehydrator and dehydrate at 90 degrees F for 24 hours.

c) After the aging is complete, open the cheese bundle and, using an ice cream scooper, remove all the cheese from the cloth and place it in the bowl of a food processor.

d) Whip until light and fluffy.

e) Adjust the seasonings to taste. If the taste is too mild, add the remaining $\frac{1}{8}$ teaspoon Celtic sea salt.

f) Turn the cheese out onto a work surface and divide it in half. Lay one half in an 8-inch piece of wax paper. Roll the cheese inside the wax paper, moving back and forth to create a log. Repeat with the second half.

g) After the shape is set, even out the ends and gently roll and press in the herbs. Gently wrap the logs in cheesecloth. Transfer to the refrigerator for 2 hours. Serve.

7.   Ahimsa goat cheese

Ingredients

- 2 cups almonds
- $3\frac{1}{2}$ teaspoons apple cider vinegar, plus more as needed
- 1 teaspoon Celtic sea salt, plus more as needed
- $\frac{1}{2}$ cup coconut milk
- 1 teaspoon refined coconut oil

Directions

a) Soak the almonds for at least 8 hours in filtered water. To sprout them, rinse the almonds with water twice a day for the next 48 hours. You can store them, covered with a piece of cheesecloth, in a cool, dry place. But make sure you drain the water from them completely each time you rinse them. Or, if desired, you can skip the sprouting step and just use soaked almonds. Your cheese will still be delicious.

b) Bring 4 cups of water to a boil in a medium saucepan over medium-high heat. Add the sprouted almonds and quickly blanch them, for 1 minute. Drain the almonds in a colander and remove the skins with your fingers.

c) In the pitcher of a Blender, place the almonds, vinegar, salt, coconut milk, and coconut oil.

Blend on medium speed, using the plunger to evenly distribute the mixture.

d) Transfer the mixture to the center of an 8-inch piece of cheesecloth. Gather the edges and tie them into a bundle with string. Place the cheesecloth bundle in the dehydrator and dehydrate at 90 degrees F for 19 to 24 hours.

e) After the aging is complete, open the cheesecloth bundle and, using an ice cream scooper, scoop the cheese into the bowl of a food processor. Whip until light and fluffy.

f) Adjust the seasonings to taste. If the taste is too mild, add another $\frac{1}{8}$ teaspoon vinegar and $\frac{1}{8}$ teaspoon salt.

g) Turn the cheese out onto wax paper. Divide the cheese into two equal parts. Roll the cheese inside the wax paper, moving back and forth to create two individual logs.

h) Enjoy with my Beet Goat Cheese Salad or with your favorite gluten-free crackers.

8.   Gorgonzola blue cheese

Ingredients

- 4 cups raw cashews
- Coconut oil, for greasing the molds
- 1 capsule acidophilus (3-billion-active-culture strain)
- $\frac{3}{4}$ cup coconut milk
- 1 teaspoon Himalayan salt
- $\frac{1}{4}$ to $\frac{1}{2}$ teaspoon spirulina or frozen liquid spirulina

Directions

a) Place the cashews in filtered water in a small bowl. Cover and refrigerate overnight.

b) Lightly oil two 4-inch cheese molds or one 6-inch cheese mold with coconut oil.

c) Drain the cashews. In the bowl of a Blender, place the cashews, acidophilus, coconut milk, and salt. Blend on medium speed, using the plunger to evenly distribute the mixture until smooth.

d) Transfer the mixture to a small bowl and sprinkle with the powdered spirulina or break off small chunks of live frozen spirulina and randomly drop them over the cheese mixture. Using a small rubber spatula, marble the spirulina through the mixture to create blue-green veins.

e) Transfer the mixture to the prepared cheese molds and place them in the dehydrator topped with parchment paper rounds cut to fit the tops of the molds.

f) Dehydrate at 90 degrees F for 24 hours.

g) Transfer the molds to the fridge overnight.

h) Remove the cheese from the molds and enjoy, or place the cheese inside a humidifier or wine cooler for 1 to 3 weeks. Rub the outside with fine sea salt every few days to prevent black mold from appearing. The taste of the cheese will continue to develop as it ages.

9.   Chipotle cheddar

Ingredients

- 1½ cups raw cashews
- 1/4 cup Irish moss
- ½ cup filtered water
- 1 teaspoon refined coconut oil
- ½ teaspoon chipotle chili from a jar, plus 1 tablespoon oil from the jar
- ½ teaspoon Celtic sea salt, plus more to taste
- 2 tablespoons nutritional yeast

Directions

a) Place the cashews in filtered water in a small bowl. Cover and refrigerate overnight.

b) Rinse the Irish moss very well in a colander until all the sand is removed and the smell of the ocean is gone. Then place it in water in a small bowl. Cover and refrigerate overnight.

c) Drain the Irish moss and place it in the bowl of a Blender with the water. Blend on high speed for 1 minute or until it is emulsified. Measure out 2 tablespoons and reserve the rest.

d) Drain the cashews. In a clean pitcher of a Blender, place the cashews, the emulsified Irish moss, the coconut oil, chipotle chili, chipotle oil, salt, and nutritional yeast. Blend on

medium speed, using the plunger to evenly
distribute the ingredients until smooth.

e) Adjust the salt to taste. Spoon the mixture
into the center of your tamale before wrapping.

10.   Cashew bleu cheese

Ingredients

- 2 cups raw cashews
- 1/4 cup Irish moss
- $\frac{1}{2}$ cup filtered water
- 1 tablespoon nutritional yeast $1\frac{1}{2}$ teaspoons Celtic sea salt
- 2 teaspoons refined coconut oil
- 1 teaspoon garlic powder
- 1 capsule acidophilus (3-billion-active-culture strain)
- 1/4 cup aquafaba (water from a 15.5-ounce can of garbanzo beans)
- $\frac{1}{2}$ teaspoon powdered spirulina or frozen live spirulina

Directions

a) Place the cashews in filtered water in a small pitcher. Cover and refrigerate overnight.

b) Rinse the Irish moss very well in a colander until all of the sand is removed and the smell of the ocean is gone. Then place it in filtered water in a small bowl. Cover and refrigerate overnight.

c) Drain the Irish moss and place it in the bowl of a Blender along with the water. Blend on high speed for 1 minute or until it is emulsified.

Measure out 2 tablespoons and reserve the rest.

d) Drain the cashews. In a clean pitcher of the Blender, place the cashews, emulsified Irish moss, the nutritional yeast, salt, coconut oil, garlic powder, acidophilus, and aquafaba.

e) Blend on medium speed, using the plunger to evenly distribute the mixture. Transfer the mixture to a cheese mold.

f) Sprinkle the spirulina over the cheese and, using a small spatula, marble it through in all directions. Do not overmix or your cheese will turn green.

g) Place the cheese mold in the dehydrator and dehydrate at 90 degrees F for 24 hours. Refrigerate overnight.

h) Serve, or store in a humidifier or wine cooler for up to 3 weeks.

11. Vegan Burrata

Ingredients

- 2 cups raw almonds
- 1 tablespoon apple cider vinegar
- 1 teaspoon Himalayan salt
- 1/4 cup coconut milk plus 1 cup for soaking
- 1 teaspoon coconut oil

Directions

a) Soak the almonds for at least 8 hours in filtered water. To sprout them, rinse the almonds with filtered water twice a day for the next 48 hours. You can store them, covered with a piece of cheesecloth, in a cool, dry place. But make sure you drain the water from them completely each time you rinse them. Or if desired you can skip the sprouting step and just use soaked almonds. Your cheese will still be delicious.

b) Bring 4 cups of water to a boil in a medium saucepan over medium-high heat. Add the almonds and quickly blanch them, for 1 minute. Drain the almonds in a colander and remove the skins with your fingers (you can compost them).

c) In the pitcher of a Blender, place the almonds, vinegar, salt, $\frac{1}{2}$ cup coconut milk, and the coconut oil. Blend on medium speed, using the plunger to evenly distribute the mixture until well incorporated and smooth.

d) Transfer the ingredients to the center of an 8-inch piece of fine cheesecloth. Gather the edges and tie them into a bundle with string. Hang the cheese bundle on a hook on the wall or on the underside of a cabinet. Place a small dish beneath it to catch the liquid. Hang overnight or until a soft darkened rind forms.

e) Place the cheesecloth bundle in a small bowl and add the remaining 1 cup of coconut milk. Cover and soak in the refrigerator for 3 to 5 days.

f) Before serving, cut the cheese into slices and arrange on some fresh greens with diced tomatoes. Try pouring 1 tablespoon of the soaking coconut milk right over the top of the slices. Drizzle some high-quality olive oil and balsamic vinegar over your gourmet creation, garnish with some fresh ground pepper, and serve.

12.   Japanese miso cheese

Ingredients

- 1 cup raw cashews
- 1 cup fresh coconut meat from a brown coconut (do not substitute with coconut flakes)
- ⅔ cup aquafaba (liquid from canned garbanzo beans)
- 1 tablespoon coconut oil, plus more for greasing the cheese molds
- 2 fermented black garlic cloves
- 1 tablespoon chickpea miso paste
- 1 tablespoon nutritional yeast
- 1 teaspoon apple cider vinegar
- 1 small seaweed sprig, any variety
- Pinch of large-grain Celtic sea salt

Directions

a) Place the cashews in filtered water in a small bowl. Cover and refrigerate overnight.

b) In the bowl of a food processor pulse the fresh coconut pieces until mealy in texture. Cover and refrigerate until ready to use.

c) Lightly oil one 4-inch round cheese mold with coconut oil.

d) Drain the cashews. In the pitcher of a Blender, place the cashews, coconut, aquafaba, and coconut oil. Blend on medium speed, using the plunger to evenly distribute the mixture until well incorporated and smooth. You may have to stop and scrape down the sides with a rubber spatula and then start again.

e) Transfer the cheese to the prepared cheese mold. Place the cheese mold in the dehydrator and dehydrate at 90 degrees F for 24 hours.

f) Remove the cheese from the mold and place in the bowl of a food processor. Add the garlic, miso, nutritional yeast, and vinegar. Process for 1 minute or until smooth. Transfer the mixture to a small decorative serving dish. Alternatively, transfer it into the prepared mold and refrigerate for 24 hours.

13. Whipped cashew ricotta

Ingredients

- 2 cups raw cashews
- 1/4 cup Irish moss
- $\frac{3}{4}$ cup filtered water
- 1 teaspoon rejuvelac
- 2 teaspoons fresh lemon juice
- 2 tablespoons aquafaba
- 1 teaspoon Celtic sea salt

Directions

a) Place the cashews in filtered water in a small bowl. Cover and refrigerate overnight.

b) Rinse the Irish moss very well in a colander until all of the sand is removed and the smell of the ocean is gone. Then place it in water in a small bowl. Cover and refrigerate overnight.

c) Drain the Irish moss and place it in the pitcher of a Blender with $\frac{1}{2}$ cup water. Blend on high speed for 1 minute or until it is emulsified. Measure out 2 tablespoons and reserve the rest.

d) In a clean bowl of the Blender, place the cashews, emulsified Irish moss, rejuvelac, remaining $\frac{1}{4}$ cup water, and salt. Blend on medium speed, using the plunger to evenly distribute the mixture, stopping and starting until everything is well incorporated.

e) Transfer the cheese to the center of an 8-inch piece of fine cheesecloth. Gather the edges and tie them into a bundle with string.

f) Place the cheesecloth bundle in the dehydrator and dehydrate at 90 degrees F for 24 hours.

g) Transfer the cheese to the bowl of a food processor and pulse until the texture is light and fluffy.

14.   Coconut cashew cheese

Ingredients

- 2 cups raw cashews
- 2 tablespoons coconut oil, plus more for greasing the cheese molds
- 2 cups fresh coconut meat from a brown coconut (do not substitute with coconut flakes)
- 1/4 cup aquafaba (liquid from canned garbanzo beans)
- 1 teaspoon Himalayan salt Edible flower petals, for garnish

Directions

a) Place the cashews in filtered water in a small bowl. Cover and refrigerate overnight.

b) Lightly oil two 4-inch cheese molds with coconut oil.

c) In the bowl of a food processor, place the coconut and pulse until mealy in texture. Set aside.

d) Drain the cashews. In the pitcher of a Blender place the cashews, coconut, aquafaba, salt, and coconut oil. Blend on medium speed, using the plunger to evenly distribute the mixture until smooth.

e) You may need to stop the blender and scrape down the sides using a rubber spatula a few times.

f) Transfer the mixture to the prepared cheese molds. Cover the molds with parchment paper rounds cut to fit the molds.

g) Place the cheese molds in the dehydrator and dehydrate at 90 degrees F for 24 hours. Refrigerate overnight.

h) Remove the cheese from the molds. Arrange on plates and decorate with edible flower petals.

CLASSIC CHEESE

15. Mascarpone

MAKES 12 ounces

Ingredients

- 2 cups pasteurized heavy cream without thickeners
- 1 cup powdered skim milk
- 1 lemon, cut in half

Directions

a) In a nonreactive, heavy 2-quart saucepan with a lid, whisk together the cream and powdered milk. Place over low heat and slowly bring to 180°F, stirring constantly to prevent scorching. It should take about 40 minutes to come to temperature. Turn off the heat.

b) Slowly squeeze the juice from half of the lemon into the cream. Switch to a metal spoon and keep stirring; do not use a whisk, as that will inhibit the curd formation. Watch carefully to see if the cream starts to coagulate. You will not see a clean break between curds and whey. Rather, the cream will coat the spoon and you will start to see some solids in the cream.

c) Add the juice from the remaining lemon half and stir with the spoon to incorporate. Cover the pan and cool the cream in the refrigerator for 8 hours or overnight.

d) When the cream is firm to the touch, transfer it to a bowl or colander lined with clean, damp butter muslin. Draw the ends together and twist into a ball to squeeze out the excess moisture. This last step will make the mascarpone thick.

16. Low-fat panir

MAKES 12 to 14 ounces

Ingredients

- 2½ quarts reduced fat (2 percent) pasteurized or raw cow's milk
- 5 cups buttermilk, homemade (see variation on Crème Fraîche) or store-bought
- 1 teaspoon sea salt

Directions

a) Put the reduced fat milk in a nonreactive, heavy 4-quart stockpot over medium-low heat and slowly bring it to 175°F to 180°F. It should take about 40 minutes to come to temperature. Turn off the heat.

b) Pour in the buttermilk and gently stir with a whisk just to combine. Coagulation will start to occur immediately, and the curds will begin to form after about 2 minutes. Slowly raise the temperature to 195°F, gently stirring with a spatula. You will see an obvious separation of curds and whey. Using a rubber spatula, gently stir until the majority of the coating curds have attached to the larger mass, about 10 more minutes. Remove from the heat and gently stir around the edge of the curds with the rubber spatula. Cover and allow the milk to ripen for 5 minutes.

c) Place a nonreactive strainer over a nonreactive bowl or bucket large enough to capture the whey. Line it with clean, damp butter muslin and gently ladle the curds into it. Make a draining sack: Tie two opposite corners of the butter muslin into a knot and repeat with the other two corners.

d) Slip a dowel or wooden spoon under the knots to suspend the bag over the whey-catching receptacle, or suspend it over the kitchen sink using kitchen twine tied around the faucet. Let the curds drain for 5 minutes, then open the cloth, distribute the salt over the curds, and gently toss the curds with your hands to incorporate. Tie closed and let drain for 10 minutes more, or until the whey stops dripping. Discard the whey or reserve it for another use.

e) While curds are still hot, open the cloth and shape the curds into a brick about $\frac{3}{4}$ to 1 inch thick. Wrap the curds snugly in the same cloth to hold the shape. Place the packet of curds on a draining rack set over a tray and set the weight on top. Press and drain for at least 30 minutes, or longer for a drier cheese.

f) Remove the cloth. The cheese will be dry and will have formed into a solid brick. If you are not using it the same day, tightly wrap the cheese in plastic wrap and store refrigerated for up to 4 days or vacuum-seal and freeze for up to 2 months.

17. Queso blanco

MAKES 1 pound

Ingredients

- 1 gallon pasteurized whole cow's milk
- About ⅓ cup cider vinegar or distilled white vinegar
- 1 teaspoon kosher salt

Directions

a) Heat the milk in a nonreactive, heavy 6-quart stockpot over medium heat to 195°F, stirring occasionally to prevent the milk from scorching. It should take about 25 to 30 minutes to bring the milk to temperature. Turn off the heat.

b) Stir in ⅓ cup vinegar using a whisk. Cover, remove from the heat, and let sit for 10 minutes. The milk protein will coagulate into solid curds and the liquid whey will be almost clear and light green in color. Depending upon the milk used, if the whey is still a bit cloudy or there are small bits of curd visible in the whey, you may need to add a bit more vinegar to fully coagulate the curds. If so, add 1 teaspoon at a time and stir the vinegar in with a rubber spatula until the remainder of the curds are formed.

c) Place a nonreactive strainer over a nonreactive bowl or bucket large enough to capture the whey. Line it with clean, damp butter muslin and gently ladle the curds into it. Let the curds drain for 5 minutes.

d) Distribute the salt over the curds and gently toss the curds with your hands to incorporate. Be careful not to break up the curds in this process.

e) Make a draining sack: Tie two opposite corners of the butter muslin into a knot and repeat with the other two corners. Slip a dowel or wooden spoon under the knots to suspend the bag over the whey-catching receptacle, or suspend it over the kitchen sink using kitchen twine tied around the faucet. Let the curds drain for 1 hour, or until the whey has stopped dripping. Discard the whey or reserve it for another use.

f) Remove the solid mass of cheese from the cloth and place in an airtight container or wrap tightly in plastic wrap and refrigerate until ready to use.

18.   Whole milk ricotta

MAKES 1 pound

Ingredients

- 1 gallon pasteurized or raw whole cow's milk
- ½ cup heavy cream
- 1 teaspoon citric acid powder
- 2 teaspoons kosher salt

Directions

a) In a non-reactive, heavy 6-quart stockpot, combine the milk, cream, citric acid, and 1 teaspoon of the salt and mix thoroughly with a whisk. Place over medium-low heat and slowly heat the milk to 185°F to 195°F. This should take about 15 to 20 minutes. Stir frequently with a rubber spatula to prevent scorching.

b) As the milk reaches the desired temperature, you will see the curds start to form. When the curds and whey separate and the whey is yellowish green and just slightly cloudy, remove from the heat. Gently run a thin rubber spatula around the edge of the curds to rotate the mass. Cover the pan and let the curds set without disturbing for 10 minutes.

c) Place a nonreactive strainer over a nonreactive bowl or bucket large enough to capture the whey. Line it with clean, damp butter muslin and gently ladle the curds into it. Use a long-handled mesh skimmer to capture the last of the curds. If any curds are stuck to the bottom of the pan, leave them there. You don't want scorched curds unflavoring your cheese.

d) Distribute the remaining 1 teaspoon salt over the curds and gently toss the curds with your hands to incorporate. Be careful not to break up the curds in the process.

e) Make a draining sack: Tie two opposite corners of the butter muslin into a knot and repeat with the other two corners. Slip a dowel or wooden spoon under the knots to suspend the bag over the whey-catching receptacle, or suspend it over the kitchen sink using kitchen twine tied around the faucet.

f) Let the curds drain for 10 to 15 minutes, or until the desired consistency has been reached. If you like moist ricotta, stop draining just as the whey stops tipping.

g) If you like it drier or are using it to make ricotta salata, let the curds drain for a longer period of time. Discard the whey or keep it for another use.

h) Transfer the cheese to a lidded container. Cover and store, refrigerated, for up to 1 week.

19.   Whey ricotta

MAKES 3 cups

Ingredients

- 1-gallon fresh cow's milk whey from making a cow's milk cheese using 2 gallons of milk
- 1 gallon pasteurized whole cow's milk
- $3\frac{1}{2}$ tablespoons distilled vinegar
- 1 tablespoon sea salt
- 1 cup pasteurized heavy cream without additives

Directions

a) Assemble a water bath using a 10-quart stockpot set inside a larger pot. Pour water into the larger pot to come two-thirds of the way up the side of the smaller pot. Remove the smaller pot and place the pot of water over low heat.

b) When the water reaches the boiling point (212°F), put the smaller pot back in the water to warm slightly, then pour the whey into the smaller pot. Gently stir the whey with a whisk using an up-and-down motion for 20 strokes to evenly distribute the heat.

c) Add the cow's milk, cover the pot, and slowly warm the milk to 192°F over the course of about 20 minutes, lowering the heat, adding cool water to the water bath, or removing from the heat if the temperature is rising too quickly.

d) Slowly pour the vinegar over the surface of the milk. Using a whisk, thoroughly incorporate the vinegar into the milk using an up-and-down motion for 20 strokes. Small curds will begin to form.

e) Cover the pot and let stand for 10 to 15 minutes, stirring once around the edge of the curds with a rubber spatula. The curds will settle down into the pot. Ladle o the whey until you can see the curds.

f) Place a nonreactive strainer over a nonreactive bowl or bucket large enough to capture the whey. Line it with clean, damp butter muslin and gently ladle the curds into it. Let the curds drain for 10 minutes. Distribute the salt over the curds and gently toss the curds with your hands to incorporate. Be careful not to break up the curds in this process. Discard the whey or reserve it for another use.

g) Transfer the ricotta to a bowl and gently mix in the cream using a rubber spatula, being careful not to break up the curds. Serve while warm, or refrigerate for up to 3 days

20. Cabécou

MAKES Four 1½- to 2-ounce disks

Ingredients

- 2 quarts pasteurized goat's milk
- ¼ teaspoon MA 011 or C20G powdered mesophilic starter culture
- 1 drop liquid rennet diluted in 5 tablespoons cool nonchlorinated water
- 2 teaspoons kosher salt
- 1 tablespoon herbes de Provence
- 2 teaspoons whole mixed peppercorns
- 4 bay leaves
- About 4 cups fruity extra-virgin olive oil

Directions

a) Assemble a water bath using a nonreactive 4-quart stockpot set inside a larger pot. Pour water into the larger pot to come halfway up the side of the smaller pot. Remove the smaller pot and place the pot of water over low heat.

b) When the water reaches 85°F, put the smaller pot back in the water to warm slightly, then pour the milk into the smaller pot. Gently mix the milk with a whisk using an up-and-down motion for 20 strokes to evenly distribute the heat.

c) Cover and slowly warm the milk to 75°F over the course of about 10 minutes, lowering the heat, adding cool water to the water bath, or removing from the heat if the temperature is rising too quickly.

d) When the milk is at temperature, remove it from the heat. Sprinkle the starter over the milk and let it rehydrate for 5 minutes. Using a whisk, stir the starter into the milk to incorporate, using an up-and-down motion for 20 strokes. Add the diluted rennet to the milk, whisking with an up-and-down motion for 20 strokes to incorporate.

e) Cover and allow the milk to set at 72°F for 18 hours, until it coagulates. During maturation, do not touch or move the milk. The curds will form a solid mass during this period.

f) Set 4 molds on a draining rack set over a tray and, using a ladle or skimmer, scoop the curds into the molds. When the molds are full, cover the rack with a kitchen towel or lid and let drain at room temperature.

g) After 2 days of draining, the cheeses will have sunk down to about 1 inch in height. Unmold them; they should be Firm enough to maintain their shape. Salt the cheeses on both sides and dry them in the lower portion of the refrigerator for 2 days on mesh cheese mats, turning once a day. Keep them uncovered, as they need to air-dry until the surface is dry to the touch.

h) Place each disk of cheese in a sterilized glass jar. Divide the herbes de Provence, peppercorns, and bay leaves among the jars and cover the cheeses with olive oil. Close the lids tightly. The olive oil will preserve the cheese, add its own flavor, and carry the Flavor of the herbs. Age for 1 week to let the flavor develop; use within 3 weeks.

21. Real cream cheese

MAKES 1½ pounds

Ingredients

- 1 quart pasteurized whole cow's milk
- 1 quart pasteurized heavy cream
- ¼ teaspoon MA 4001 powdered mesophilic starter
- 2 drops calcium chloride diluted in 2 tablespoons cool nonchlorinated water
- 3 drops liquid rennet diluted in 2 tablespoons nonchlorinated water
- 1 teaspoon kosher salt

Directions

a) Assemble a water bath using a non-reactive 4-quart pot set inside a larger pot.

b) Heat the milk and cream in the smaller pot until it reaches 75°F, stirring occasionally. This should take about 15 minutes. Turn off the heat.

c) Sprinkle the starter over the milk and let it rehydrate for 5 minutes. Whisk the starter into the milk to incorporate, using an up-and-down motion for 20 strokes. Add the diluted calcium chloride and incorporate in the same way, and then the diluted rennet. Cover, remove from the water bath, and let sit at room temperature for 12 hours, or until solid curds form and liquid whey Goats on top. The whey will be almost clear and light green in color.

d) Place a nonreactive strainer over a nonreactive bowl or bucket large enough to capture the whey. Line it with clean, damp butter muslin and gently ladle the curds into it. Tie the ends of the muslin to fashion a draining sack and let drain for 6 to 8 hours, or until firm to the touch. Discard the whey or reserve it for another use.

e) Transfer the curds to a bowl, add the salt, and stir or knead to combine. Form into a brick and wrap with plastic wrap or store in a covered container. Refrigerate for up to 2 weeks.

22. Créme Fraîche Cottage Cheese

Ingredients

- 1 gallon pasteurized whole cow's milk
- $\frac{3}{8}$ teaspoon Aroma B powdered mesophilic starter culture
- 1 teaspoon calcium chloride diluted in $\frac{1}{4}$ cup cool nonchlorinated water (omit if using raw milk)
- 1 teaspoon liquid rennet diluted in $\frac{1}{4}$ cup cool nonchlorinated water
- 1 teaspoon kosher salt
- 1 to $1\frac{1}{2}$ cups crème fraîche, homemade or store-bought

Directions

a) Assemble a water bath using a 6-quart stockpot set inside a larger pot. Pour water into the larger pot to come two-thirds of the way up the side of the smaller pot. Remove the smaller pot and place the pot of water over low heat.

b) When the water reaches 80°F, put the smaller pot back in the water to warm slightly, and then pour the milk into the smaller pot. Cover the pot and slowly warm the milk to 70°F over the course of about 15 minutes, lowering the heat, adding cool water to the water bath, or removing from the heat if the temperature is rising too quickly.

c) When the milk is at temperature, sprinkle the starter over the milk and let it rehydrate for 5 minutes. Whisk the starter into the milk to incorporate, using an up-and-down motion for 20 strokes. Add the diluted calcium chloride and incorporate in the same way, and then the diluted rennet. Cover, remove from the water bath, and let sit at room temperature for 3 to 4 hours. The milk protein will coagulate into solid curds, and the liquid whey will be almost clear and light green in color.

d) Check the curds for a clean break, using a sanitized long-blade curd cutting knife or 10-inch cake decorating spatula. If the cut edge is clean and there's some accumulation of light-colored whey in the cut area, the curds are ready. If the cut edge is soft and the curds are mushy, the curds are not ready; allow them to sit longer before testing again. When ready, cut the curds into ¾-inch pieces and gently stir using a rubber spatula for 5 minutes to Firm up the curds slightly.

e) Return the pot to the water bath over low heat and slowly bring the temperature of the curds to 115°F, raising the temperature about 5°F every 5 minutes. This will take about 40 minutes.

f) During this time, gently stir the curds two or three times to expel more whey and firm them up slightly. When the curds are near temperature, half- fill a large bowl with cold water and ice and line a colander or strainer with clean, damp butter muslin. When the curds are at temperature, they should be Firm and bean-sized. Ladle the curds into the cloth-lined colander and immediately set the colander in the ice water bath. This will set up the curds and stop them from ripening any further.

g) Let the curds drain completely in the colander, about 15 minutes, then toss with the salt until evenly combined. Gently fold in enough crème fraîche to coat the curds. The cheese may be refrigerated for up to 10 days.

23. Crescenza

Ingredients

- 2 gallons pasteurized whole cow's milk
- 1 teaspoon Aroma B powdered mesophilic starter culture
- 1 teaspoon calcium chloride diluted in $\frac{1}{4}$ cup cool nonchlorinated water
- 1 teaspoon liquid rennet diluted in $\frac{1}{4}$ cup cool nonchlorinated water Kosher salt Nonchlorinated water, chilled to 55°F

Directions

a) In a nonreactive, heavy 10-quart stockpot, heat the milk over low heat to 90°F. This should take about 20 minutes.

b) Sprinkle the starter over the milk and let it rehydrate for 5 minutes. Whisk the starter into the milk to incorporate, using an up-and-down motion for 20 strokes. Cover and, maintaining the temperature at 90°F, allow the milk to ripen for 30 minutes.

c) Add the diluted calcium chloride and incorporate in the same way, then add the diluted rennet.

d) Cover and let sit at room temperature for 45 minutes, or until the curds are firm and there is a clean break between curds and whey.

e) Cut the curds into 1-inch pieces and let rest for 10 minutes. Gently stir with a rubber spatula for 5 minutes to firm up the curds slightly. Allow the curds to settle to the bottom of the pot. Ladle enough whey to expose the tops of the curds.

f) Place a Taleggio mold on a draining rack set over a tray and line the mold with clean, damp butter muslin. Gently ladle the soft curds into the mold, cover the curds with the tails of the muslin, and let drain for 3 hours at room temperature. Lift the cloth sack from the mold, unwrap the cheese, dip it over, and return it to the cloth. Place the sack back in the mold and let drain for another 3 hours, then remove the cheese from the cloth.

g) In a food-grade container with a lid, make enough brine to cover the

unwrapped cheese by combining 1-part
salt with 5 parts of the chilled water.
Place the cheese in the brine for 2 hours
at room temperature, Whipping the
cheese after 1 hour to ensure even salt
absorption.

h) Remove the cheese from the brine, pat
dry, and place on the draining rack to
further drain and air-dry for 1 hour at
room temperature, or until the surface
is dry to the touch.

i) Wrap thoroughly in plastic wrap or
vacuum-seal and refrigerate until ready
to use. This cheese is best when
consumed within 1 week of wrapping,
though if vacuum-sealed it can keep for
up to 1 month.

24. Basic chèvre

Ingredients

- 1 gallon pasteurized goat's milk
- 1 teaspoon C20G powdered mesophilic starter culture
- 1 teaspoon sea salt

Directions

a) In a nonreactive, heavy 6-quart stockpot, heat the milk over low heat to 86°F. This should take 18 to 20 minutes. Turn off the heat.

b) When the milk is at temperature, sprinkle the starter over the milk and let it rehydrate for 5 minutes. Whisk the starter into the milk to incorporate, using an up-and-down motion for 20 strokes.

c) Cover and, maintaining the temperature between 72°F and 78°F, allow the milk to ripen for 12 hours.

d) The curds are ready when they have formed one large mass in the pot with the consistency of thick yogurt, surrounded by clear whey. Place a nonreactive strainer over a nonreactive bowl or bucket large enough to capture the whey. Line it with a single layer of clean, damp butter muslin and gently ladle the curds into it. Let drain for 5 minutes, then gently toss the curds with the salt.

e) At this point you can cover the curds with the tails of the muslin and leave to drain over the bowl, or you can spoon the curds into 2 chèvre molds set on a draining rack set over a tray. Let drain at room temperature for 6 hours for creamy cheese, or 12 hours if you wish to shape the cheese. If you are using the molds,

f) Remove the cheese from the cheesecloth or molds and place in a covered container. Use right away, or store refrigerated for up to 1 week.

GOAT CHEESES

25. Fromage blanc

MAKES 1½ pounds

Ingredients

- 1 gallon pasteurized reduced fat (2 percent) cow's milk ¼ teaspoon MA 4001 powdered mesophilic starter culture
- 4 drops calcium chloride diluted in 2 tablespoons cool nonchlorinated water (omit if using raw milk)
- 4 drops liquid rennet diluted in 2 tablespoons cool nonchlorinated water
- 1 teaspoon kosher salt

Directions

a) Assemble a water bath using a 6-quart stockpot set inside a larger pot. Pour water into the larger pot to come two-thirds of the way up the side of the smaller pot. Remove the smaller pot and place the pot of water over low heat.

b) When the water reaches 85°F, put the smaller pot back in the water to warm slightly, then pour the milk into the smaller pot. Cover the pot and slowly warm the milk to 75°F over the course of about 15 minutes, lowering the heat, adding cool water to the water bath, or removing from the heat if the temperature is rising too quickly. Turn off the heat.

c) When the milk is at temperature, sprinkle the starter over the milk and let it rehydrate for 5 minutes. Whisk the starter into the milk to incorporate, using an up-and-down motion for 20 strokes.

d) Add the diluted calcium chloride and incorporate in the same way, then add the diluted rennet in the same way. Cover and let set at room temperature for 12 hours, or until the curds are solid and the whey is almost clear and yellowish in color.

e) Place a nonreactive strainer over a nonreactive bowl or bucket large enough to capture the whey. Line it with clean, damp butter muslin and gently ladle the curds into it. Make a draining sack or leave the curds to drain in the colander for 4 to 6 hours, or until the desired consistency is achieved. Discard the whey or reserve it for another use.

f) Transfer the curds to a bowl and sprinkle with the salt, then whisk to combine. Use right away, or store refrigerated for up to 2 weeks.

26. Queso fresco

MAKES 2 pounds

Ingredients

- 2 gallons pasteurized whole cow's milk
- 1 teaspoon Meso II powdered mesophilic starter culture
- 1 teaspoon calcium chloride diluted in $\frac{1}{4}$ cup cool nonchlorinated water (omit if using raw milk)
- 1 teaspoon liquid rennet diluted in $\frac{1}{4}$ cup cool nonchlorinated water
- $1\frac{1}{2}$ teaspoons kosher salt

Directions

a) In a nonreactive, heavy 10-quart stockpot, heat the milk over medium heat to 90°F, stirring occasionally with a rubber spatula to prevent scorching. This should take about 20 minutes. Turn off the heat.

b) When the milk is at temperature, sprinkle the starter over the milk and let it rehydrate for 5 minutes. Whisk the starter into the milk to incorporate, using an up-and-down motion for 20 strokes. Cover and maintain the temperature at 90°F for 30 minutes to ripen the milk.

c) Add the diluted calcium chloride and gently incorporate with a whisk using an up-and-down motion for 1 minute. Add the diluted rennet and incorporate in the same way. Cover and maintain the 90°F temperature for 45 minutes more, or until the curds give a clean break when cut with a knife.

d) Cut the curds into ¼-inch pieces and let them set for 10 minutes. Return the uncovered pot to low heat and gradually increase the temperature to 95°F over 20 minutes, gently stirring the curds a few times to keep them from matting. Remove the pot from the heat and let the curds settle for 5 minutes, then ladle on enough whey to expose the curds.

e) Place a nonreactive strainer over a nonreactive bowl or bucket large enough to capture the whey. Line it with clean, damp butter muslin and gently ladle the curds into it. Let drain for 5 minutes. Distribute the salt over the curds and gently toss to incorporate, being careful not to break up the curds in the process.

f) Lift the cloth full of curds from the strainer and place it into the 5-inch tomme mold. Using your hands, distribute the curds evenly in the mold. Cover the curds with the tails of the cloth and set the follower in place, then place in a press at 8 pounds of pressure for 6 hours at room temperature. You may also use a 1-gallon container full of water for the weight.

g) Remove the cheese from the mold and the cloth and use right away, or store refrigerated in a covered container for up to 2 weeks.

27.   Quark

MAKES 1½ pounds

Ingredients

- 2 quarts pasteurized whole cow's milk
- 2 quarts pasteurized reduced fat (2 percent) cow's milk
- 1 teaspoon Aroma B powdered mesophilic starter culture
- 1 teaspoon calcium chloride diluted in ¼ cup cool nonchlorinated water
- 1 teaspoon liquid rennet diluted in ¼ cup cool nonchlorinated water
- 1½ teaspoons kosher salt

Directions

a) In a nonreactive 6-quart stockpot slowly heat both milks over low heat to 72°F. This should take about 15 minutes. Turn off the heat.

b) When the milk is at temperature, sprinkle the starter over the milk and let it rehydrate for 5 minutes. Whisk the starter into the milk to incorporate, using an up-and-down motion for 20 strokes. Cover and, maintaining the temperature at 72°F, allow the milk to ripen for 30 minutes.

c) Add the diluted calcium chloride and gently stir with a whisk using an up-and-down motion for 1 minute. Add the diluted rennet and incorporate in the same way.

d) Cover and let sit at room temperature for 12 to 18 hours, until the whey is coating on top and the curds give a clean break when cut with a knife. If the cut edge is clean and there's some accumulation of light-colored whey in the cut area, the curds are ready. If the cut edge is soft and the curds are mushy, the curds are not ready; allow them to sit 10 minutes longer before testing again.

e) Slowly return the curds and whey to 72°F over low heat. Cut the curds into $\frac{1}{2}$-inch pieces, remove from the heat, and gently stir for 5 minutes. Let the curds rest and sink to the bottom of the pot, maintaining temperature. Ladle whey until the curds are exposed, then ladle the curds into a colander lined with clean, damp butter muslin. Let the curds drain for 6 to 10 hours, or until the desired moisture level is achieved; longer draining will result in drier quark.

f) Transfer the curds to a bowl and toss with the salt, gently folding it in using a rubber spatula. Let drain for another 5 minutes if excess whey exists. Use right away, or store refrigerated in a covered container for up to 2 weeks.

SALT-RUBBED AND BRINED CHEESES

28. Cotija

MAKES $1\frac{3}{4}$ pounds

Ingredients

- 2 gallons pasteurized whole cow's milk
- 1 teaspoon Meso II powdered mesophilic starter culture
- 1 teaspoon Thermo B powdered thermophilic starter culture
- 1 teaspoon calcium chloride diluted in $\frac{1}{4}$ cup cool nonchlorinated water
- 1 teaspoon liquid rennet diluted in $\frac{1}{4}$ cup cool nonchlorinated water
- Kosher salt

Directions

a) In a nonreactive 10-quart stockpot over low heat, slowly heat the milk to 100°F, stirring occasionally to prevent scorching. This should take about 25 minutes. Turn off the heat.

b) When the milk is at temperature, sprinkle the starters over the milk and let it rehydrate for 5 minutes. Whisk the starters into the milk to incorporate, using an up-and-down motion for 20 strokes. Cover and, maintaining the temperature at 100°F, let the milk ripen for 30 minutes.

c) Add the diluted calcium chloride to the milk and incorporate using the same up-and-down technique, then add the diluted rennet in the same way.

d) Cover and maintain the temperature at 100°F for 1½ hours, or until the curds give a clean break when cut.

e) Continuing to maintain the curds at 100°F, cut them into ½-inch pieces and let sit for minutes. Slowly raise the temperature to 105°F over 10 minutes, gently stirring around the edge of the pot with a rubber spatula and moving the curds continuously to form up the surface and prevent them from matting. The curds will expel whey and shrink to the size of lentils. Let the curds rest for 10 minutes, still maintaining 105°F.

f) Place a nonreactive strainer over a nonreactive bowl or bucket large enough to capture the whey. Line it with clean, damp butter muslin and gently ladle the curds into it. Let drain for 15 minutes, or until the whey stops dripping. Distribute $1\frac{1}{2}$ teaspoons of salt over the curds and use your hands to gently toss the curds to incorporate, being careful not to break up the curds in the process

g) Place the 5-inch tomme mold on a draining rack set over a baking sheet. Line the mold with damp cheesecloth or butter muslin. Gently transfer the drained curds to the lined cheese mold, cover with the tails of the cloth, and set the follower on top of the curds. Press at 15 pounds for 30 minutes. Remove the cheese from the mold and peel away the cloth, tip the cheese over, and redress. Press again at the same pressure for 8 hours or overnight.

h) Two or more hours before you'll need it, make the brine by combining $1\frac{1}{2}$ cups of salt and 1 quart of water in a noncorrosive bucket or a container with a lid; chill to 50°F to 55°F.

i) Remove the cheese from the mold and unwrap it, then place it in the brine. Let it soak at 50°F to 55°F for 24 hours, tipping it over after 12 hours to evenly distribute the brine.

j) Remove the cheese from the brine and pat dry. Air-dry for 6 hours, then place on a cheese mat in a ripening box. Age at 55°F at 80 to 85 percent humidity, turning daily. Remove any unwanted mold with cheesecloth dampened in a vinegar-salt solution and wipe down the box to maintain humidity.

k) After 2 weeks, wrap the cheese in cheese paper and store in your refrigerator for up to 4 more weeks. Alternately, vacuum-seal the cheese and refrigerate for up to 2 months.

29. Ricotta salata

MAKES 12 ounces

Ingredients

- 1 gallon pasteurized whole cow's milk
- $\frac{1}{2}$ cup heavy cream
- 1 teaspoon citric acid powder
- Kosher salt

Directions

a) Follow the whole milk ricotta recipe. Add 1 tablespoon kosher salt or cheese salt to the curds and toss with your hands to distribute.

b) Line a ricotta mold with clean, damp cheesecloth and place on a draining rack set over a tray. Press the cheese into the mold, cover with the tails of the cheesecloth, and weight it down with a slightly less than 2-pound weight, such as a pint jar full of water. Press for 1 hour, then unmold the cheese, unwrap it,

c) Press it at the same weight for 12 hours or overnight.

d) Unmold and unwrap the cheese, then lightly rub the surface with kosher or cheese salt. Redress the cheese with clean cheesecloth, return it to the mold, set it on a drying rack in a ripening box, and refrigerate for 12 hours.

e) Take the cheese out of the cheesecloth, tip it over, and rub all over with more salt, then return the undressed cheese to the mold.

f) Continue this process of tipping and salting once a day for 7 days to pull out moisture and assist in the curing process. After 3 days, remove the cheese from the mold and keep aging it on the rack. If any unwanted mold appears, wipe it o with cheesecloth dampened in a vinegar-salt solution.

g) After 1 week, or when the desired firmness has been reach, brush any excess salt from the surface, cover, and age the cheese in the refrigerator until the desired texture is achieved. Use right away, or wrap in cheese paper and store in the refrigerator for at least 2 weeks and up to 2 months.

30. Feta

Ingredients

- 1 gallon pasteurized goat's milk
- 1 teaspoon mild lipase powder diluted in $\frac{1}{4}$ cup cool nonchlorinated water 20 minutes before using
- 1 teaspoon Aroma B powdered mesophilic starter culture
- 1 teaspoon liquid calcium chloride diluted in $\frac{1}{4}$ cup cool nonchlorinated water
- $\frac{1}{2}$ teaspoon liquid rennet diluted in $\frac{1}{4}$ cup cool nonchlorinated water
- 2 to 4 tablespoons sea salt or kosher salt
- Kosher salt

Directions

a) In a nonreactive, heavy 6-quart stockpot, combine the milk and the diluted lipase, if using, gently whisking the lipase into the milk using an up-and-down motion for 20 strokes. Place over low heat and slowly heat the milk to 86°F. This should take 18 to 20 minutes. Turn off the heat.

b) When the milk is at temperature, sprinkle the starter over the milk and let it rehydrate for 2 minutes. Whisk the starter into the milk to incorporate, using an up-and-down motion for 20 strokes. Cover and, maintaining the temperature at 86°F, let the milk ripen for 1 hour.

c) Add the diluted calcium chloride to the ripened milk and gently stir with a whisk using an up-and-down motion for 1 minute. Add the diluted rennet and incorporate in the same way. Cover and maintain at 86°F for 1 hour, or until the curds form a solid mass with light yellow whey coating on top and show a clean break. If there is no clean break after 1 hour, test again in 15 minutes.

d) Cut the curds into $\frac{1}{2}$-inch pieces. Still maintaining a temperature of 86°F, allow them to sit undisturbed for 10 minutes. Using a rubber spatula, gently stir the curds for 20 minutes to release more whey and keep the curds from matting. The curds will look more pillow-like at the end of this process. If you want a firmer curd, raise the temperature to 90°F for this step. Let the curds rest for 5 minutes, undisturbed, still at temperature. The curds will settle to the bottom of the pot.

e) Line a colander with clean, damp cheesecloth or butter muslin and, using a slotted spoon, transfer the curds to the colander. Tie the corners of the cloth together to create a draining sack, then let drain for 2 hours, or until the whey has stopped tipping.

f) The curds should form a solid mass and feel firm; if not, let them dry for another hour. If you desire a more uniform shape, after $\frac{1}{2}$ hour of draining in the colander, transfer the sack to a square cheese mold or plastic mesh tomato basket set over a draining rack. Line the mold with the sack of curds, press the cheese out into the corners of the mold, and finish draining. Remove the cheese from the cloth and Hip it over every hour in this draining process to help even out the texture and firm up the cheese.

g) When it is drained, transfer the cheese to a bowl. Cut it into 1-inch-thick slices and then into 1-inch cubes. Sprinkle the chunks with 6ake sea salt, making sure all the surfaces are covered. Loosely cover the bowl with a lid or plastic wrap and allow to age in the salt for 5 days in the refrigerator. Check daily and pour out any expelled whey.

h) The feta can be used at this point or stored in brine for another 21 days. If the finished cheese is too salty for your taste, soak the cheese in nonchlorinated water for 1 hour, then let drain before using. Feta can be stored for a few months in brine.

31. Halloumi

MAKES 12 ounces

Ingredients

- 1 gallon pasteurized whole cow's milk
- 1 teaspoon mild lipase powder dissolved in $\frac{1}{4}$ cup cool nonchlorinated water 20 minutes before using (optional)
- 1 teaspoon calcium chloride diluted in $\frac{1}{4}$ cup cool nonchlorinated water (omit if using raw milk)
- 1 teaspoon liquid rennet diluted in $\frac{1}{4}$ cup cool nonchlorinated water
- 1 teaspoon dried mint
- Kosher salt

Directions

a) In a nonreactive, heavy 6-quart stockpot, slowly heat the milk over low heat to 90°F. This should take about 20 minutes. Turn off the heat.

b) If using lipase, gently whisk it into the milk using an up-and-down motion for 1 minute, then let rest for 5 minutes. Add the diluted calcium chloride and gently stir with a whisk using an up-and-down motion for 1 minute. Add the diluted rennet and incorporate in the same way.

c) Cover and, maintaining the temperature at 90°F, let the milk ripen for to 45 minutes, or until the curds give a clean break when cut with a knife. Still maintaining 90°F, cut the curds into $\frac{3}{4}$-inch pieces and let sit for 5 minutes.

d) Over low heat, slowly bring the curds to 104°F over a 15-minute period. The curds will break up slightly. Maintaining the 104°F temperature, gently and continuously stir with a rubber spatula for 20 minutes. The curds will shrink and firm up slightly, taking on an individual shape. Let the curds rest for 5 minutes, maintaining temperature. They will sink to the bottom and the whey will rise to the top. Ladle o enough whey to expose the top of the curds.

e) Place a nonreactive strainer over a nonreactive bowl or bucket large enough to capture the whey. Line it with clean, damp butter muslin and gently ladle the curds into it. Toss the dried mint with the curds if using, and let drain for 15 minutes, or until the whey stops tipping.

f) Place the 5-inch tomme mold on a draining rack set over a tray. Line the mold with clean, damp cheesecloth, and then gently transfer the drained curds to the mold.

g) Cover the top of the curds with the excess cheesecloth and set the follower on top. Place the mold in a cheese press or place an 8-pound weight on top of the follower and press at 8 pounds of pressure for 3 hours.

h) Remove the cheese from the mold, peel away the cheesecloth, tip the cheese over, and redress with the cheesecloth. Press again at 8 pounds for another 3 hours.

i) Remove the pressed curds from the mold and cut off the rounded edges to create a 4- inch square. Reserve the trimmings to use as a crumbled cheese topping. If the pressed curds are 2 inches thick or more, halve the slab horizontally.

j) Using a cheese making pot, slowly heat the reserved whey to 190°F over 30 minutes. Place the square or squares of curds in the hot whey and cook for 30 to 35 minutes, or until the cheese shrinks slightly and oats on the top of the whey. Be sure to maintain the temperature throughout cooking and do not let the whey boil.

k) Using a mesh skimmer, remove the cheese from the whey and place it on a draining rack to cool. Air-dry, tipping at least once, until the surfaces are dry to the touch, about 30 minutes.

l) Meanwhile, make a medium-heavy brine by combining the salt with 1 gallon of 50°F to 55°F water. Place the dried cheese in a noncorrosive container and cover with the cool brine. Store covered in the refrigerator for 5 days or up to 2 months. Save the unused brine in a labeled container at 50°F to 55°F for another brining.

STRETCHED-CURD CHEESES

32. Traditional mozzarella

MAKES 1 pound

Ingredients

- 1 gallon pasteurized whole cow's or goat's milk
- 1 teaspoon Thermo B powdered thermophilic starter culture
- 1 teaspoon calcium chloride diluted in $\frac{1}{4}$ cup cool nonchlorinated water $\frac{3}{4}$ teaspoon liquid rennet diluted in $\frac{1}{4}$ cup cool nonchlorinated water
- Kosher salt

Directions

a) In a nonreactive 6-quart stockpot, slowly heat the milk to 95°F over low heat; this should take about 20 minutes. Turn off the heat.

b) Sprinkle the starter over the milk and let it rehydrate for 5 minutes. Mix well using a whisk in an up-and-down motion for 20 strokes. Cover and maintain 90°F to 95°F, letting the milk ripen for 45 minutes. Add the diluted calcium chloride and gently whisk in. Let rest for 10 minutes. Add the diluted rennet and gently whisk in. Cover and let sit, maintaining 90°F to 95°F for 1 hour, or until the curds give a clean break.

c) Cut the curds into ½-inch pieces and let sit undisturbed for 30 minutes, maintaining at 90°F to 95°F. During this time the curds will firm up and release more whey. Over low heat, slowly raise the temperature to 105°F over 30 minutes, gently stirring from time to time and frequently checking the temperature and adjusting the heat as needed.

d) If you raise the temperature too quickly, the curds won't coagulate or bind properly. Once 105°F is reached, remove from the heat and, using a rubber spatula, gently stir for 10 minutes around the edges of the pot and under the curds to move them around. Maintaining temperature, let the curds rest for another 15 minutes; they will sink to the bottom.

e) Line a colander with damp butter muslin, set it over another pot, and scoop the curds into it with a slotted spoon. Let drain for 15 minutes, or until the curds stop dripping whey. Reserve the whey.

f) Gently return the drained curds to the original pot and place it in a 102°F to 105°F water bath. Hold the water bath temperature for 2 hours. The curds will melt into each other, binding into a slab; turn the slab two times during this period, using a spatula.

g) When 2 hours have elapsed, begin testing the curds' pH using a pH meter or pH strips. Check the pH every 30 minutes during this period; once it drops below 5.6, check it every minutes, as it will fall rapidly after this point. Once the pH drops into the 4.9 to 5.2 range, the curds are ready to stretch.

h) Transfer the curds to a warm strainer, let drain for a couple of minutes, then transfer to a sterilized cutting board. Cut the curds into approximately 1-inch cubes and put them in a clean stainless steel bowl large enough to hold them with plenty of room to spare (the curds will be covered with hot liquid).

i) In a clean pot, heat 4 quarts of water or of the reserved whey to 170°F to 180°F. Pour this over the curds to cover them completely.

j) Wearing heat-resistant gloves, work the submerged cubes of curd into one large ball, kneading and shaping it in the hot water. Once the curds are shaped into a Warm ball, lift it out of the water and, working quickly, pull and stretch it into a long rope about 18 inches long.

k) If the curd rope cools and becomes brittle, dip it into the hot water to make it warm and pliable again. Loop the rope back on itself, and then pull and stretch it again two or three times, just until the curd is shiny and smooth.

l) The curd is now ready for shaping. To shape into a ball, pinch off the amount you want to shape, stretching the surface of the ball to become tight and shiny; tuck the ends into the underside as though forming a ball of pizza dough.

m) Turn the ball over in your hand and press the underside edges up into the center of the ball, into the palm of your hand. Immediately submerge the ball in a bowl of ice water to chill and firm up for 10 minutes.

n) While the cheese is chilling, prepare a light brine. You can use the reserved whey for the brine, supplementing water as needed to equal 3 quarts, dissolving 9 ounces of kosher salt into it, and chilling it to 50°F to 55°F.

o) This results in a less salty finished cheese. For a saltier finished cheese, make 3 quarts of saturated brine and chill to 50°F to 55°F. Place the chilled cheese in the brine solution. If using the saturated brine, soak the cheese for 20 minutes, tipping it over a few times.

p) If using the weaker whey brine, you can leave the cheese in the brine, refrigerated, for up to 8 hours, tipping the cheese over a few times. Either way, remove from the brine and use immediately, or place in a plastic food storage container, cover with water, and store refrigerated for up to 1 week.

33. Burrata

MAKES 4 large pouches or 8 small
pouches

Directions

a) Prepare Traditional Mozzarella up to the
   point of stretching and shaping into a
   single smooth ball and chilling in ice
   water.

b) Prepare the Filling of your choice:
   MOZZARELLA FILLING: mozzarella
   scraps broken into small pieces and
   mixed with a small amount of cream to
   moisten

c) Divide the mozzarella into four 4-ounce
   portions, place the pieces in a bowl, and
   cover them with 170°F to 180°F water.

d) When the mozzarella is heated through
   and pliable, about 5 minutes, pull the
   pieces out of the water and quickly
   stretch them into approximately 4-inch
   squares, either cupped in the palm of
   your hand or pressed into shape on a
   cutting board. If you like, as you form
   the squares you can drape them inside a
   4-ounce stainless steel ladle to shape

into pouches; dip the ladle in the hot water if needed to keep the mozzarella elastic.

e) Once a piece of mozzarella is stretched, fill it with 1½ ounces or so of filling and quickly pull 2 opposite gaps up and over the filling to completely enclose. Bring the other 2 gaps together and pinch closed, then dip the pouch into the hot water brie y to seal.

f) Smooth the surface of the ball with the palm of your hand and place in an ice bath to cool for 2 to 3 minutes. Form and fill the other pouches. If you like, you can tie a chive around the closure before chilling.

34. Queso Oaxaca

Directions

a) To make queso Oaxaca in the style of the Mozzarella Company, make Traditional Mozzarella through to melting the curds in the hot whey. Pinch off palm-size pieces of the kneaded submerged ball of curds, then pull and stretch the hot pieces into 1-inch-wide ribbons about 2 feet long.

b) Lay the thin ribbons out at on a work surface in one continuous back-and-forth rope of curds—like ribbon candy. Generously salt the warm ribbons with kosher salt and leave it for 5 minutes. Then squeeze the juice of 1 lime over the top and gently rub the salt and lime juice into the ribbons.

c) Leave for 10 minutes, then wind the ribbons into yarn-like balls

d) Make 2 quarts of light brine, cooled to 50°F to 55°F. Immerse the balls in the brine for 15 minutes, then remove and let drain for 30 minutes before wrapping in plastic wrap and refrigerating overnight, or for up to 10 days.

35. Bocconcini

Directions

a) To make bocconcini, follow the recipe for Traditional Mozzarella to the point when you have cut the curds into cubes and heated the whey, but have not poured the hot whey over the cubes.

b) Place a handful of cubed curds into a skimmer or slotted spoon and, wearing heat-resistant gloves, dip the utensil into the hot whey for several seconds, melting the curds until they're stretchable.

c) Using a spoon or your fingers, and working quickly, knead the melted curds in the utensil, dripping it back into the hot whey as needed to keep the curds pliable.

d) When the curds are kneaded into a firm ball, pull and stretch them into a small rope and fold them over onto themselves, repeating a few times until the ball of curds is smooth, pliable, and shiny. Don't overwork the curds, or you'll toughen the cheese.

e) Form the curds into a bite-size ball shape and place it in a bowl of ice water for 10 minutes to chill and firm up. Repeat with the rest of the curds until all are stretched and shaped into balls.

f) Make a brine with the hot whey by dissolving 6 ounces of kosher salt in it and adding water to make 2 quarts of brine, then chill it to 50°F to 55°F.

g) Place the chilled cheese in the whey brine for 2 hours. Use immediately for best flavor, or store in the salted whey, covered and refrigerated, for up to 1 week.

36. Junket mozzarella

MAKES 1 pound

Ingredients

- 1 gallon pasteurized but not homogenized whole cow's milk
- 7 tablespoons distilled vinegar (5 percent acidity)
- 4 tablets junket rennet dissolved in ½ cup cool nonchlorinated water
- 1½ teaspoons plus ¼ cup kosher salt (

Directions

a) In a nonreactive 6-quart stockpot, slowly heat the milk to 88°F over low heat; this should take about 20 minutes. Stir in the vinegar using a whisk in an up-and-down motion to incorporate thoroughly. Add the dissolved rennet and gently whisk in for 1 minute.

b) Slowly raise the temperature to 90°F over 8 minutes. Remove from the heat, cover, and let sit, maintaining the temperature for 1 hour, until the curds form a solid mass of bonded small curds the consistency of soft tofu. A few small curds may be coating in the clear, yellow whey. Check for a clean break, and if there isn't a clean break, check again in 15 minutes.

c) Cut the curds into $\frac{1}{2}$-inch pieces and let sit undisturbed for 10 minutes, maintaining them at 90°F. Over low heat, raise the temperature to 108°F over 15 minutes, gently stirring every 5 minutes and frequently checking the temperature and adjusting the heat as needed. If you raise the temperature too quickly, the curds won't coagulate and bind properly.

d) Once 108°F is reached, remove from the heat and, using a rubber spatula, gently stir for 10 minutes around the edges of the pot and under the curds to move them around and expel more whey. Let the curds rest for another 15 minutes. At this point the curds will be slightly below the surface of the whey.

e) Gently press one of the curds between two fingers. It should feel springy and stretchable; if it doesn't, leave the curds for 10 minutes and then test again.

f) Line a colander with damp butter muslin, set it over another pot, and scoop the curds into it with a slotted spoon. Let drain for 15 minutes, or until the whey has stopped dripping and the curds are compacted together. Reserve the whey.

g) Add the $1\frac{1}{2}$ teaspoons of salt to the whey and stir to dissolve. Slowly heat the whey over medium-low heat to 175°F to 180°F; this should take about 30 minutes.

h) Meanwhile, wrap the muslin over the curds and place the packet on a cutting board. Flatten the curds slightly and let sit for 20 minutes. Open the muslin and cut the slab of curds into $\frac{1}{2}$-inch strips or chunks.

i) Place a handful of curd strips or chunks in a skimmer or slotted spoon and, wearing heat-resistant gloves, dip the utensil into the hot whey for several seconds, melting the curds until stretchable.

j) Using a spoon or your fingers, and working quickly, knead the melted curds in the utensil, tipping it back into the hot whey as needed to keep the curds pliable. When the curds are kneaded into a firm ball, pull and stretch them into a small rope and fold them over onto themselves, repeating a few times until the ball of curds is smooth, pliable, and shiny.

k) Don't overwork the curds, or you'll toughen the cheese. Shape the curds into a ball and place it in a bowl of ice water for 10 minutes to chill and firm up. Repeat the melting, kneading, stretching, shaping, and chilling with the remaining curd strips.

l) Make a light brine by dissolving the $\frac{1}{4}$ cup of kosher salt in the hot whey, then chill it to 50°F to 55°F. Place the chilled cheese in the brine for 2 hours. Use immediately for best flavor, or store in the salted whey, covered and refrigerated, for up to 1 week.

37. Braided string cheese

MAKES 1 pound

Ingredients

- 1 gallon pasteurized low-fat (1 percent) or reduced fat (2 percent) cow's milk
- 1 teaspoon Thermo B powdered thermophilic starter culture
- 1 teaspoon calcium chloride diluted in $\frac{1}{4}$ cup cool nonchlorinated water
- $\frac{3}{4}$ teaspoon liquid rennet diluted in $\frac{1}{4}$ cup cool nonchlorinated water
- Kosher salt

Directions

a) In a nonreactive 6-quart stockpot, slowly heat the milk to 95°F; this should take about 25 minutes. Turn off the heat.

b) Sprinkle the starter over the milk and let it rehydrate for 5 minutes. Mix well using a whisk in an up-and-down motion. Cover and maintain 90°F to 95°F, letting the milk ripen for 45 minutes.

c) Add the diluted calcium chloride and gently whisk in. Let rest for 10 minutes.

Add the diluted rennet and gently whisk in. Cover and let sit, maintaining 90°F to 95°F for 1 hour, or until the curds give a clean break.

d) Cut the curds into $\frac{1}{2}$-inch pieces and let sit undisturbed for 30 minutes, maintaining a

e) 90°F to 95°F temperature. During this time the curds will firm up and release more whey. Over low heat, slowly raise the temperature to 105°F over 30 minutes, gently stirring and frequently checking the temperature and adjusting the heat as needed.

f) If you raise the temperature too quickly, the curds won't coagulate and bind properly. Once 105°F is reached, remove from the heat and, using a rubber spatula, gently stir for 10 minutes around the edges of the pot and under the curds to move them around.

g) Maintaining temperature, let the curds rest for another 15 minutes; they will sink to the bottom.

h) Using a skimmer or slotted spoon, transfer the curds to a colander or strainer, reserving 5 inches of whey in the pot.

i) Place the colander of curds over the pot. Over low heat, heat the whey in the pot to 102°F to 105°F over the course of minutes. Cover the curds in the colander with the pot lid while the whey is heating; more whey will drain into the pot below.

j) When the whey is at temperature, remove from the heat and hold at 102°F to 105°F for 2 hours. The curds will melt into each other, binding into a slab; turn the slab two times during this period, using a spatula.

k) When 2 hours have elapsed, begin testing the pH of the curds with a pH meter or pH strips every 30 minutes. Once the pH drops below 5.6, begin checking every 15 minutes. Once the pH drops into the 4.9 to 5.2 range, the curds are ready to stretch.

l) Transfer the curds to a cutting board. Cut the curds into approximately $\frac{1}{2}$-inch cubes and put them in a clean stainless steel bowl large enough to hold them with plenty of room to spare (the curds will be covered with hot liquid). In a clean pot, heat 4 quarts of water or of the reserved whey to 170°F to 180°F. Pour this over the curds to cover them completely.

m) Wearing heat-resistant gloves, work the submerged cubes of curd into one large ball, kneading and shaping it in the hot water. Once the curds are shaped into a Warm ball, lift it out of the water and, working quickly, pull and stretch it into an 8-inch-long rope.

n) If the curd cools and becomes brittle, dip it into the hot water to make it warm and pliable again.

o) Working lengthwise along the rope, pull 1-inch sections and, working quickly, pull and stretch the lengths into 1-foot-long, 1-inch-thick ropes, then fold them over onto themselves two or three times, stretching each time. The more the strips are stretched, the stringier the cheese will be. Place the stretched lengths on a cutting board.

p) Using kitchen scissors or a knife, cut the lengths into 6- to 8-inch-long pieces. In groups of 3, twist them together to look like a braid. Once they are formed, immediately place the pieces in a bowl of ice water for 5 minutes to chill and firm up.

q) Make a light brine by dissolving 6 ounces of kosher salt into all of the whey, adding water as needed to make 2 quarts and chilling it to 50°F to 55°F.

38. Bread Cheese

Directions

a) The cheese is cooked to melt and develop a thin golden crust from the fat that's brought to the surface as the slab of curds heats up. It is served with bread as a snack or warmed for breakfast.

b) To make bread cheese, make Braided String Cheese up to the point where the cut curds are melting in the bowl of hot water. Wearing heat-resistant gloves, work the melted curds into a slab big enough to fill your pan. Fold the slab over onto itself lengthwise, then stretch it out again to the size of the pan. Repeat two more times, discarding any whey that is expelled in the stretching.

c) Preheat the griddle pan over medium-high heat. Place the slab into the heated pan and cook to melt slightly and form a golden crust on the bottom of the cheese. Using a spatula, tip it over and brown the other side for about 5 minutes.

d) Remove from the heat and let the cheese cool slightly in the pan. Remove from the pan and cut into slices and serve while still warm. Bread cheese can be vacuum-sealed or wrapped tightly in foil and refrigerated for up to 3 months.

e) To serve, reheat it in a 350°F oven or under the broiler.

39. Kasseri

MAKES Two 1-pound cheeses

Ingredients

- 5 quarts pasteurized whole cow's milk
- 2 quarts pasteurized goat's milk
- 1 quart pasteurized half-and-half
- $\frac{1}{4}$ teaspoon Thermo B powdered thermophilic starter culture
- 1 teaspoon mild lipase powder dissolved in $\frac{1}{4}$ cup cool nonchlorinated water 20 minutes before using
- 1 teaspoon calcium chloride diluted in $\frac{1}{4}$ cup cool nonchlorinated water (omit if using all raw milk)
- 1 teaspoon liquid rennet diluted in $\frac{1}{4}$ cup cool nonchlorinated water
- Kosher salt

Directions

a) Combine the milks and half-and-half in a 10-quart stockpot set in a 108°F water bath over low heat. Bring the milk to 98°F over 12 minutes. Turn off the heat.

b) Sprinkle the starter over the milk and let it rehydrate for 5 minutes. Mix well using a whisk in an up-and-down motion. Cover and maintain 98°F, letting the milk ripen for 45 minutes. Add the dissolved lipase and gently whisk in. Let sit for 10 minutes. Add the diluted calcium chloride and gently whisk in for 1 minute. Let sit for 5 minutes. Add the diluted rennet and gently whisk in for 1 minute. Cover and let sit, maintaining 98°F for 45 minutes, or until the curds give a clean break.

c) Using a whisk, gently cut the curds into bean-size pieces and let sit undisturbed for 10 minutes, maintaining 98°F. This helps firm up the curds. Over low heat, slowly raise the temperature of the water bath so that the milk comes to 104°F over 30 minutes.

d) Gently stir from time to time and frequently check the temperature and adjust the heat as needed. If you raise the temperature too quickly, the curds won't coagulate and bind properly.

e) Once 104°F is reached, remove from the heat and, using a rubber spatula, gently stir for 10 minutes around the edges of the pot and under the curds to move them around. Maintaining temperature, let the curds rest for another 15 minutes; they will sink to the bottom.

f) Line a colander with damp butter muslin, set it over another pot, and scoop the curds into it with a slotted spoon. Let the curds drain for 15 to 20 minutes, or until they have stopped dripping.

g) Lift the cloth and curds out of the colander and place on a cutting board. Using your hands, compress the curds into a rectangular shape and wrap the cloth around it to secure. Place the bundle of curds on a draining rack set over a tray, cover the bundle with another tray, and place a 3-pound weight on top. Press and let drain at room temperature for 6 to 7 hours or overnight at 50°F to 55°F.

h) Heat 3 quarts of water to 175°F. Open the bundle of curds and cut the slab into 1-inch slices. Place the slices in the pot of 175°F water.

i) Let sit for 30 seconds or so to heat through, then, wearing heat-resistant gloves, check the curds for readiness by skimming a slice of curd out and pressing and kneading it with your fingers. Hold one end of the piece and let it stretch from its own weight, then pull on it to stretch it into a string. If this stretching happens easily, the curds are ready to be shaped. If the stretching does not happen easily, keep the curds in the hot water until they are easily stretchable.

j) Still wearing heat-resistant gloves, work the submerged slices of curd into a large ball, kneading and stretching until the ball is smooth. Lift the ball out of the water and, working quickly, press it into two 5-inch square or rectangular cheese molds. If the curds cool and become brittle while you are working them, dip the mass into the hot water to make it warm and pliable again.

k) Place the molds on a draining rack set over a pan and let the curds drain for 2 hours at room temperature, tipping the cheeses two or three times by taking them out of the molds, turning them over, and replacing them in the molds.

l) Cover the draining pan and mold with a lid or kitchen towel to keep the cheeses warm and let drain for 12 hours at room temperature. This process will release more whey, which should be drained o periodically.

m) Remove the cheeses from their molds and place them on a cheese mat on a draining rack set over a pan. Rub the tops of the cheeses with salt and let them drain for 2 hours at room temperature.

n) Flip the cheeses over and rub the unsalted tops. Let them drain for 24 hours at room temperature. Repeat the process one more time: salting, draining for 2 hours, salting, and draining for 24 hours.

o) Gently rinse the salt over the cheeses with cool water. Pat the cheeses dry with a paper towel, then place them on a cheese mat in a ripening box at 65°F and 85 percent relative humidity.

p) Turn the cheeses daily for 1 week, wiping off any unwanted mold with cheesecloth dampened in a vinegar-salt solution and wiping down the sides of the box. Flip the cheeses twice weekly thereafter. Age for 2 to 4 months. When aged to your taste, wrap the cheeses in foil and refrigerate for up to 2 more months.

40. Provolone

MAKES 1 pound

Ingredients

- 1 gallon pasteurized whole cow's or goat's milk
- 1 teaspoon Thermo B powdered thermophilic starter culture
- 1 teaspoon sharp lipase powder dissolved in $\frac{1}{4}$ cup cool nonchlorinated water 20 minutes before using
- 1 teaspoon calcium chloride diluted in $\frac{1}{4}$ cup cool nonchlorinated water
- 1 teaspoon liquid rennet diluted in $\frac{1}{4}$ cup cool nonchlorinated water Kosher salt

Directions

a) In a nonreactive 6-quart stockpot, slowly heat the milk to 97°F over low heat; this should take about 25 minutes. Turn off the heat.

b) Sprinkle the starter over the milk and let it rehydrate for 5 minutes. Mix well using a whisk in an up-and-down motion.

Cover, let sit, and maintain 97°F, letting the milk ripen for 45 minutes. Add the diluted lipase and gently whisk in. Let rest for 10 minutes. Add the diluted calcium chloride and gently whisk in.

c) Add the diluted rennet and gently whisk in. Cover and let sit, maintaining 97°F for 1 hour, or until the curds give a clean break.

d) Cut the curds into $\frac{1}{2}$-inch pieces and let sit undisturbed for 30 minutes, maintaining 97°F. Over low heat, slowly raise the temperature to 108°F over 35 minutes. Gently stir from time to time and frequently check the temperature and adjust the heat as needed. If you raise the temperature too quickly, the curds won't coagulate and bind properly.

e) Once 108°F is reached, remove from the heat and, using a rubber spatula, gently stir for 10 minutes around the edges of the pot and under the curds to move them around. Maintaining temperature, let the curds rest for another 15 minutes; they will sink to the bottom.

f) Using a skimmer or slotted spoon, transfer the curds to a colander or strainer set over another pot and let them drain for 10 minutes, or until the whey stops dripping. Pour the whey from the original pot into the new pot and set it aside.

g) Gently return the drained curds to the original pot and set it in a 112°F to 115°F water bath to bring the curds to 102°F to 105°F. Hold the temperature of the curds at 102°F to 105°F for 2 hours. The curds will melt into each other, binding into a slab; turn the slab two times during this period, using a spatula.

h) When 2 hours have elapsed, begin testing the pH of the curds with a pH meter or pH strips every 30 minutes. Once the pH drops below 5.6, begin checking every 15 minutes. Once the pH drops into the 4.9 to 5.2 range, the curds are ready to stretch.

i) Transfer the curds to a strainer, let drain for 10 minutes, then place on a cutting board. Cut the curds into 1-inch cubes and put them in a stainless steel bowl large enough to hold them with plenty of room to spare (the curds will be covered with hot liquid). In a clean pot, heat 4 quarts of water or of the reserved whey to 170°F to 180°F and pour it over the curds to cover completely.

j) Wearing heat-resistant gloves, work the submerged cubes of curd into one large ball, kneading and shaping it in the hot water. Once the curds are shaped into a Warm ball, lift it out of the water and, working quickly, pull and stretch it into a 1-foot-long rope. If the curd rope cools and becomes brittle, dip it into the hot water to make it warm and pliable again.

k) Loop the rope back on itself, and then pull and stretch it again two or three times, or until the curd is shiny and smooth.

l) Pinch the amount of curd you want to shape. If shaping a ball, stretch the surface of the ball to become tight and shiny; tuck the ends into the underside as though forming a ball of pizza dough. Once the cheese is formed into the desired shape, immediately submerge it in a bowl of ice water for 10 minutes to chill and Warm up.

m) Remove the shaped cheese or cheeses from the water and set aside to air-dry while making the brine.

41. Smoked Scamorza

Directions

a) Follow the recipe for Traditional Mozzarella through the point when the curds have been kneaded and stretched until shiny and smooth.

b) Pinch the amount of cheese you want to shape. One of the traditional shapes looks like a small hourglass, with a small knob at the top and a larger bulbous bottom. The top is shaped from one-third of the ball, with the bottom being the larger portion.

c) While the curds are malleable, place the ball of hot stretched curds into the palm of your hand. Using your thumb and fore finger, gently squeeze the ball to form a $1\frac{1}{2}$-inch-diameter neck about one-third down from the top, rotating while shaping.

d) Then put the cheese into an ice bath for 1 hour to firm up the shape. Drain, then wrap the neck, leaving a tail to hang the cheese, as is traditional.

SEMISOFT, FIRM, AND HARD CHEESES

42. Dill havarti

MAKES 2 pounds

Ingredients

- 2 gallons pasteurized whole cow's milk
- 1 teaspoon MM 100 powdered mesophilic starter culture
- 1 teaspoon calcium chloride diluted in $\frac{1}{4}$ cup cool nonchlorinated water
- 1 teaspoon liquid rennet diluted in $\frac{1}{4}$ cup cool nonchlorinated water
- 4 teaspoons kosher salt
- 1 teaspoon dried dill

Directions

a) In a nonreactive 10-quart stockpot, heat the milk over low heat to 70°F; this should take about 12 minutes.

b) Sprinkle the starter over the milk and let it rehydrate for 5 minutes. Mix well using a whisk in an up-and-down motion for 1 minute. Cover and maintain 70°F, letting the milk ripen for 45 minutes. Add the calcium chloride and gently whisk in for 1 minute. Slowly raise the heat to 86°F over 7 to 8 minutes, then add the rennet and gently whisk in for 1 minute. Cover and let sit, maintaining 86°F for 30 to 45 minutes, or until the curds give a clean break.

c) Still maintaining 86°F, cut the curds into ½-inch pieces and let sit for 5 minutes. Gently stir the curds for 10 minutes, then let sit for 5 minutes. Ladle out about one-third of the whey (this should be about 2½ quarts) and add 3 cups of 130°F water. When the temperature of the curds and whey reaches 92°F to 94°F, add another 3 cups of 130°F water.

d) Gently stir for 5 minutes, then add another 2 cups of 130°F water. Add the salt and stir to dissolve. Check the temperature and add 130°F water as needed to bring the curds and whey to about 97°F. Continue stirring until the curds feel springy in your hand when squeezed, about 20 minutes. Ladle enough whey to expose the curds. Gently stir in the dill.

e) Line an 8-inch tomme mold (with follower) with damp butter muslin and place it on a draining rack. Gently ladle the curds into the mold and press them in with your hands. Pull the cloth tight and smooth, removing any wrinkles. Fold the cloth tails over the curds, set the follower on top, and press at 8 pounds for 30 minutes.

f) Remove the cheese from the mold, peel away the cloth, tip the cheese over, and redress with the same cloth. Press again at 8 pounds, redressing every 30 minutes for up to 3 hours, or until the whey stops draining.

g) Leave the cheese in the mold without pressure for about 3 more hours before putting in the refrigerator for 12 hours or overnight. Remove the cheese from the mold. It is now ready to eat, or it can be aged for more intense flavor.

h) Make 2 quarts of saturated brine in a noncorrosive container with a lid and chill it to 50°F to 55°F. Submerge the cheese in the brine and soak at 50°F to 55°F for 8 hours or overnight.

i) Remove the cheese from the brine and pat dry. Air-dry at room temperature on a rack for 12 hours, then age at 55°F and 85 percent humidity on a cheese mat set in a ripening box, [tipping daily. Age for 1 month, or longer if desired, removing any unwanted mold with cheesecloth dampened in a vinegar-salt solution.

43.   Edam boule

MAKES Two 1-pound boules

Ingredients

- 2 gallons pasteurized reduced fat (2 percent) cow's milk
- $\frac{1}{2}$ teaspoon Meso II or MM 100 powdered mesophilic starter culture
- 1 teaspoon liquid annatto coloring diluted in ⅓ cup cool nonchlorinated water
- 1 teaspoon calcium chloride diluted in $\frac{1}{4}$ cup cool nonchlorinated water
- 1 teaspoon liquid rennet diluted in $\frac{1}{4}$ cup cool nonchlorinated water Kosher salt

Directions

a) In a nonreactive 10-quart stockpot, heat the milk over low heat to 88°F; this should take about 15 minutes.

b) Sprinkle the starter over the milk and let it rehydrate for 5 minutes. Mix well using a whisk in an up-and-down motion. Cover and maintain 88°F, letting the milk ripen for 30 minutes. Add the annatto and gently whisk in for 1 minute. Add the calcium chloride and gently whisk in for 1 minute, then add the rennet in the same way. Cover and let sit, maintaining 88°F for 30 to 45 minutes, or until the curds give a clean break.

c) Cut the curds into ½-inch pieces and let sit for 5 minutes. Over low heat, slowly raise the temperature to 92°F over 15 minutes. Gently and frequently stir to keep the curds from matting together. The curds will release more whey, firm up slightly, and shrink to the size of small peanuts.

d) Once 92°F is reached, remove from the heat, maintain the temperature, and let the curds rest undisturbed for 30 minutes; they will sink to the bottom. Ladle out enough whey to expose the curds and reserve the whey.

e) Stir the curds continuously for 20 minutes, or until they are matted and cling together when pressed in your hand. Add just enough warm water (about 2 cups) to bring to 99°F, then maintain the temperature for 20 minutes. The curds will settle again.

f) Place a strainer over a bowl or bucket large enough to catch the whey. Line it with damp butter muslin and ladle the curds into it. Let the curds drain for 5 minutes, then toss with 1 tablespoon of salt. Divide the curds into 2 portions, placing each portion on damp muslin and tying the corners of the muslin to create tight sacks around the curds.

g) Shape the curds into balls within the muslin and hang to let drain for 30 minutes, or until the whey stops tipping.

h) Place the reserved whey in the cheese pot and heat over medium heat to 122°F. Take the boules of curds out of the cloth and submerge them in the warm whey for 20 minutes, maintaining the temperature. Turn the boules a few times to ensure even heating. Redress the boules in their cloth sacks, then hang to let drain and air-dry at room temperature for 6 hours.

i) Make 2 quarts of medium brine in a noncorrosive container with a lid and cool to 50°F to 55°F. Remove the cheeses from the cloth. Place in the brine, cover, and soak overnight at 50°F to 55°F.

j) Remove the cheeses from the brine and pat dry. Air-dry at room temperature on a cheese mat for 1 to 2 days, or until the surface is dry to the touch.

k) Wax the cheese using liquid wax and then cheese wax. Ripen at 50°F to 55°F and 85 percent humidity for 2 to 3 months, tipping the cheese daily for even ripening. Age 6 months for optimum flavor, maintaining 50°F to 55°F and 85 percent humidity.

44. Fontina

MAKES One 1½-pound cheese or two 12-ounce cheeses

Ingredients

- 2 gallons pasteurized whole cow's milk
- ½ teaspoon Meso II or MM 100 powdered mesophilic starter culture
- 1 teaspoon mild lipase powder diluted in ¼ cup cool nonchlorinated water 20 minutes before using
- 1 teaspoon calcium chloride diluted in ¼ cup cool nonchlorinated water
- 1 teaspoon liquid rennet diluted in ¼ cup cool nonchlorinated water
- Kosher salt for brining

Directions

a) In a nonreactive 10-quart stockpot, heat the milk over low heat to 88°F; this should take about 20 minutes.

b) Sprinkle the starter over the milk and let it rehydrate for 5 minutes. Mix well using a whisk in an up-and-down motion for 20 strokes. Cover and maintain 88°F, letting the milk ripen for 30 minutes. Add the lipase and gently whisk in for 1 minute. Add the calcium chloride and gently whisk in for 1 minute, then add the rennet in the same way. Cover and let sit, maintaining 88°F for 45 to 50 minutes, or until the curds give a clean break.

c) Still maintaining 88°F, cut the curds into pea-size pieces and stir for 10 minutes. Maintaining temperature, let the curds rest undisturbed for 30 minutes; they will sink to the bottom of the pot.

d) Heat 1 quart of water to 145°F and maintain that temperature. Ladle enough whey to expose the curds. Ladle in enough hot water to bring the temperature to 102°F.

e) Stir the curds continuously for 10 minutes, or until they are matted and cling together when pressed in your hand. The curds will be half their original size at this point. Again, ladle enough whey to expose the curds.

f) Line an 8-inch tomme mold (with follower) or 2 fresh cheese molds with damp butter muslin and place on a draining rack. Pack the drained curds into the mold or molds. Pull the cloth up tight and smooth around the curds, cover with the tails of damp muslin (and the follower if using the tomme mold), and press at 5 pounds for 15 minutes.

g) Remove the cheese from the mold, unwrap the cloth, tip the cheese over, and redress, then press at 10 to 20 pounds for 8 hours.

h) Make 2 quarts of medium-heavy brine in a noncorrosive container with a lid and cool to 50°F to 55°F. Remove the cheese from the mold or molds and cloth.

i) Place in the brine and soak at 50°F to 55°F, covered, for 12 hours, tipping a few times during that time.

j) Remove the cheese from the brine and pat dry. Air-dry at room temperature on a cheese mat for 1 to 2 days.

k) Place on a rack in a ripening box and ripen at 55°F to 60°F and 90 to 95 percent humidity for at least 2 months, tipping the cheese daily for even ripening.

l) After 3 days, wipe the cheese with a simple brine solution, then repeat every 2 days for 1 month. Continue to wipe and tip twice a week for the duration of the ripening time: from 2 months to 6 months or longer, maintaining 55°F to 60°F and 90 to 95 percent humidity.

45. Gouda

MAKES 1½ pounds

Ingredients

- 2 gallons pasteurized whole cow's milk
- ¼ teaspoon Meso II powdered mesophilic starter culture
- 1 teaspoon calcium chloride diluted in ¼ cup cool nonchlorinated water
- 1 teaspoon liquid rennet diluted in ¼ cup cool nonchlorinated water
- Kosher salt

Directions

a) Heat the milk in a 10-quart stockpot set in a 96°F water bath over low heat. Bring the milk to 86°F over 15 minutes. Turn off the heat.

b) Sprinkle the starter over the milk and let it rehydrate for 5 minutes. Mix well using a whisk in an up-and-down motion.

c) Cover and maintain 86°F, allowing the milk to ripen for minutes. Add the calcium chloride and gently whisk in for 1 minute, then add the rennet and gently whisk in for 1 minute. Cover and let sit, maintaining 86°F for 30 to 45 minutes, or until the curds give a clean break.

d) Still maintaining 86°F, cut the curds into $\frac{1}{2}$-inch pieces and let sit for 5 minutes. Stir for 5 minutes, then let sit for 5 more minutes.

e) Heat 2 quarts of water to 140°F and maintain that temperature. When the curds sink to the bottom of the pot, ladle o 2 cups of whey, then add enough 140°F water to bring the curds to 92°F (start with 2 cups). Gently stir for 10 minutes, then let the curds settle again.

f) Ladle enough whey to expose the top of the curds, then add enough 140°F water to bring the curds to 98°F (start with 2 cups). Holding the curds at that temperature, gently stir for 20 minutes, or until the curds have shrunk to the size of small beans. Let the curds settle for 10 minutes; they will knit together in the bottom of the pot.

g) Line an 8-inch tomme mold (with follower) with damp butter muslin and place it on a draining rack. Warm a colander with hot water. Drain off the whey and transfer the knitted curds to the warm colander. Let drain for 5 minutes.

h) Using your hands, break o 1-inch chunks of curd and distribute into the cloth-lined mold, filling the mold with all of the curds.

i) Press the curds into the mold with your hands as you go. Pull the cloth up tight and smooth around the curds, cover with the tails of the cloth and the follower, and press at 10 pounds for 30 minutes. Remove the cheese from the mold, unwrap the cloth, tip the cheese over, and redress, then press at 15 pounds for 6 to 8 hours.

j) Make 2 quarts of medium-heavy brine in a noncorrosive container with a lid and cool to 50°F to 55°F. Remove the cheese from the mold and cloth. Place in the brine and soak at 50°F to 55°F for 8 hours or overnight.

k) Remove the cheese from the brine and pat dry. Place on a rack and air-dry at room temperature for 1 to 2 days, or until the surface is dry to the touch.

l) Place on a mat in a ripening box, cover loosely, and age at 50°F to 55°F and 85 percent humidity for 1 week, turning daily. Remove any unwanted mold with cheesecloth dampened in a vinegar-salt solution.

m) Coat the cheese with wax and age at 55°F for 1 month and up to 6 months.

46. Jack cheese

MAKES 2 pounds

Ingredients

- 2 gallons pasteurized whole cow's milk
- 1 teaspoon MA 4001 powdered mesophilic starter culture
- 1 teaspoon calcium chloride diluted in $\frac{1}{4}$ cup cool nonchlorinated water
- 1 teaspoon liquid rennet diluted in $\frac{1}{4}$ cup cool nonchlorinated water
- 2 tablespoons kosher salt

Directions

a) In a nonreactive 10-quart stockpot, heat the milk over low to 86°F; this should take about 15 minutes. Turn off the heat.

b) Sprinkle the starter over the milk and let it rehydrate for 5 minutes. Mix well using a whisk in an up-and-down motion. Cover and maintain 86°F, allowing the milk to ripen for 1 hour. Add the calcium chloride and gently whisk in for 1 minute. Add the rennet and gently whisk in for 1 minute. Cover and let sit, maintaining

86°F for 30 to 45 minutes, or until the curds give a clean break.

c) Still maintaining 86°F, cut the curds into $\frac{3}{4}$-inch pieces and let sit for 5 minutes. Over low heat, slowly bring the curds to 102°F over 40 minutes, stirring continuously to keep the curds from matting together. They will release whey, firm up slightly, and shrink to the size of dried beans.

d) Maintain 102°F and let the curds rest undisturbed for 30 minutes; they will sink to the bottom. Ladle out enough whey to expose the curds. Stir continuously for 15 to 20 minutes, or until the curds are matted and cling together when pressed in your hand.

e) Place a colander over a bowl or bucket large enough to capture the whey. Line it with damp butter muslin and ladle the curds into it. Let drain for 5 minutes. then sprinkle in 1 tablespoon of the salt and mix thoroughly with your hands.

f) Draw the ends of the cloth together and twist to form a ball to help squeeze out the excess moisture. Roll the ball on a surface to release more whey. Tie the top of the cloth sack, press with your hands to flatten slightly, and place on a cutting board sitting on top of a draining rack. Put a second cutting board on top of the flattened sack, place an 8-pound weight directly over the cheese, and press into a wheel at 75°F to 85°F for 6 hours for moist Jack or 8 hours for firmer Jack.

g) Remove the cheese from the sack and pat dry. Rub the entire surface with the remaining 1 tablespoon of salt and place the cheese back on the draining rack to air-dry.

h) Dry at room temperature for 24 hours, or until the surface is dry to the touch, tipping once.

i) Place the cheese on a mat in a ripening box and ripen at 50°F to 55°F and 80 to 85 percent humidity for 2 to 6 weeks, tipping daily.

j) When the desired ripeness is reached, vacuum-seal or wrap well in plastic wrap and refrigerate until ready to eat. Once opened, this cheese will dry out and harden over time, creating a wonderful grating cheese.

HAND MADE CHEESE

47. Just jack

MAKES 1 pound

Ingredients

- 1 gallon pasteurized whole cow's milk
- 1 cup pasteurized heavy cream
- 1 teaspoon Meso III powdered mesophilic starter culture
- 1 teaspoon calcium chloride diluted in $\frac{1}{4}$ cup cool nonchlorinated water
- 1 teaspoon liquid rennet diluted in $\frac{1}{4}$ cup cool nonchlorinated water
- 1 tablespoon kosher salt
- 2 ounces butter or lard at room temperature

Directions

a) In a nonreactive 6-quart stockpot, heat the milk and cream over low heat to 89°F; this should take about 20 minutes. Turn off the heat.

b) Sprinkle the starter over the milk and let it rehydrate for 5 minutes. Mix well using a whisk in an up-and-down motion.

Cover and maintain 89°F, letting the milk ripen for 45 minutes. Add the calcium chloride and gently whisk in for 1 minute. Add the rennet and gently whisk in for 1 minute. Cover and let sit, maintaining 89°F for 35 minutes, or until the curds give a clean break.

c) Maintaining 86°F to 89°F, cut the curds into ½-inch pieces and let rest for 10 minutes. Over low heat, slowly bring the curds to 101°F over 35 minutes, stirring frequently to keep the curds from matting. They will release whey, firm up slightly, and shrink to the size of dried beans.

d) Ladle o enough whey to expose the curds and continue to stir for 45 to 60 minutes, keeping the temperature between 98°F and 100°F. Ladle out most of the whey and add enough 50°F water to bring the curd temperature down to 79°F. Let rest at that temperature for 4 minutes.

e) Place a colander over a bowl or bucket large enough to capture the whey. Line it with damp cheesecloth and ladle the curds into it. Keep the curds broken up for 30 minutes by gently using your hands to keep the curds from knitting together, then sprinkle in the salt. Using your hands, toss the curds and salt together for 5 minutes.

f) Line a 5-inch mold with damp cheesecloth and place it on a draining rack. Ladle the curds into the mold, let drain for 10 minutes, then pull the cloth tight and smooth.

g) Fold the cloth tails over the curds, place the follower on top, and press at 1 pound for at least 15 minutes. Remove from the mold, unwrap the cheesecloth, tip the cheese over, and redress, then press at 4 pounds for at least 10 hours. Remove the cheese from the mold and let it air-dry at 50°F to 55°F and 80 to 85 percent humidity for 24 hours. This will set up the surface for rind development.

h) Rub the cheese with the butter or lard, then bandage with cheesecloth and age at 55°F and at 65 to 75 percent humidity for at least 2 months, tipping it every other day. When the desired ripeness is reached, vacuum-seal or wrap well in plastic wrap and refrigerate until ready to eat. Opened, the cheese will dry out and harden over time, creating a wonderful grating cheese.

48. Alpine-style tomme

MAKES 2 pounds

Ingredients

- 2 gallons pasteurized whole cow's milk
- 1 teaspoon Meso II powdered mesophilic starter culture
- 1 teaspoon Thermo C powdered thermophilic starter culture
- 1 teaspoon calcium chloride diluted in $\frac{1}{4}$ cup cool nonchlorinated water
- 1 teaspoon liquid rennet diluted in $\frac{1}{4}$ cup cool nonchlorinated water
- 1 tablespoon kosher salt, plus more for brining

Directions

a) In a nonreactive 10-quart stockpot, heat the milk over low heat to 70°F; this should take about 10 minutes. Turn off the heat.

b) Sprinkle the starter cultures over the milk and let rehydrate for 5 minutes.

Mix well using a whisk in an up-and-down motion. Over low heat, slowly raise the temperature to 90°F. Add the calcium chloride and gently whisk in, then add the rennet in the same way. Cover and maintain 90°F, letting the milk ripen for 45 minutes, or until the curds give a clean break.

c) Still maintaining 90°F, cut the curds to the size of small peas. Let the curds rest for 5 minutes, then gently stir for 10 minutes. You may cut the curds again if they are not uniform in size.

d) Slowly raise the temperature 1°F every 2 minutes, stirring continuously, until the curds have reached 95°F. Continuing to stir, raise the temperature a little faster —1°F every minute—until the temperature is 100°F. Holding this temperature, let the curds rest for about 5 minutes.

e) Ladle the whey to about 1 inch above the curds. Place a strainer over a bowl or bucket large enough to capture the whey. Line it with damp butter muslin and ladle the curds into it. Let drain for 10 minutes, or until the curds stop dripping whey.

f) Set an 8-inch tomme mold (with follower) on a draining rack. Place the sack of drained curds into the mold. Fold the cloth tails over the curds, set the follower on top, and press at 10 pounds for 15 minutes. Remove the cheese from the mold, unwrap the cloth, tip the cheese over, and redress. Press at 20 pounds for 15 minutes, then redress again. Continue pressing at 20 pounds for a total of 3 hours, redressing every 30 minutes.

g) Remove the cheese from the mold and let air-dry at room temperature for 8 hours or overnight. Rub the surface of the cheese with about 1 tablespoon of salt, set it on a draining rack, and cover with a damp kitchen towel.

h) Refrigerate for 5 days, re-dampening the towel every few days to keep the rind from drying out, and tipping the cheese daily. Or instead of dry salting, you can make a near-saturated brine and submerge the cheese in it for 8 hours, then pat dry and refrigerate.

i) Age at 50°F and 80 to 85 percent humidity for 2 to 4 months. If mold becomes noticeable, brush the cheese with a dedicated nailbrush or wipe with cheesecloth dampened in salt water. If the mold is persistent, you may run the cheese under trickling cold water, then let the rind air-dry, using a small fan to circulate the air, before storing again.

49. Gruyère

MAKES 1¾ pounds

Ingredients

- 2 gallons pasteurized whole cow's milk
- 1 teaspoon Thermo C powdered thermophilic starter culture
- 1 teaspoon calcium chloride diluted in ¼ cup cool nonchlorinated water
- 1 teaspoon liquid rennet diluted in ¼ cup cool nonchlorinated water
- Kosher salt

Directions

a) Heat the milk in a nonreactive 10-quart stockpot set in a 100°F water bath over low heat. Bring the milk to 90°F over 20 minutes. Turn off the heat.

b) Sprinkle the starter over the milk and let it rehydrate for 5 minutes. Mix well using a whisk in an up-and-down motion for 20 strokes. Cover and maintain 90°F, letting the milk ripen for 30 minutes. Add the calcium chloride and gently whisk in for 1 minute. Add the rennet

and gently whisk in for 1 minute. Cover
and let sit, maintaining 90°F for 30 to 40
minutes, or until the curds give a clean
break.

c) Cut the curds into $\frac{1}{4}$-inch pieces and let
sit undisturbed for 5 minutes. Over low
heat, raise the temperature slowly to
122°F over 1 hour. Remove from the heat
and gently stir for 15 minutes.

d) The curds will release whey, Firm up
slightly, and shrink to the size of
peanuts. Let the curds rest for 20
minutes. Ladle over enough whey to
expose the curds.

e) Line an 8-inch mold (with follower) with
damp cheesecloth and place on a draining
rack. Gently ladle the curds into the
mold and let drain for 5 minutes. Gently
press with your hand to compact the
curds. Pull the cheesecloth tight and
smooth. Fold the cloth tails over the
curds, place the follower on top, and
press at 8 pounds for 1 hour. Remove the
cheese from the mold, unwrap the
cheesecloth, tip the cheese over, and

redress, then press at 10 pounds for 12 hours.

f) Meanwhile, make 2 quarts of a near-saturated brine solution in a noncorrosive container and chill to 50°F to 55°F. Remove the cheese from the mold and cloth and place it in the brine at 50°F to 55°F to soak for 12 hours, tipping it over once.

g) Remove from the brine and pat dry. Place on a drying rack, cover loosely with cheesecloth, and air-dry at room temperature for 8 hours, or until the surface is dry to the touch. tip the cheese over at least one time during the drying process.

h) Place the cheese in a ripening box, cover loosely, and ripen at 54°F and 90 percent humidity, tipping daily for 1 week. Rub with a simple brine solution twice a week for 3 more weeks. The salt solution will decrease the amount of mold that grows on the surface. Age for 2 months or longer. Wrap and store in the refrigerator.

50.   Tea-Smoked Gruyère

Directions

a) In a bowl, combine ½ cup of brown sugar, ½ cup of white rice, ¼ cup of black or oolong tea leaves, and 2 whole star anise pods.

b) Line the bottom of a wok with foil, fitting it tightly along the interior. Put the tea mixture in the wok.

c) Bring the cheese to room temperature, pat it dry, and place it in a bamboo steamer basket or on a rack large enough to hold the cheese at least 2 inches above the tea mixture. Place a pan or pie tin of ice water slightly smaller in diameter than the smoking rack or steamer between the smoldering smoke source and the cheese. The water pan will act as a barrier to the heat and keep the cheese cool enough to absorb the smoke properly without melting. Prop up the water pan with wads of foil if needed.

d) Heat the wok over medium heat until the tea mixture begins to smoke. Cover the wok, reduce the heat to low, and smoke the cheese for 10 to 12 minutes. Turn off the heat and continue to smoke for another 6 to 8 minutes. Remove the cheese from the wok and set it aside to cool, then wrap and chill before serving.

e) Discard the smoking ingredients. The smoked cheese can be stored in the refrigerator for up to 1 month.

51. Jarlsberg

MAKES $1\frac{3}{4}$ pounds

Ingredients

- 7 quarts pasteurized whole cow's milk
- 1 quart pasteurized low-fat (1 percent) milk
- 1 teaspoon Thermo C powdered thermophilic starter culture
- $\frac{1}{8}$ teaspoon propionic bacteria powder
- 1 teaspoon calcium chloride diluted in $\frac{1}{4}$ cup cool nonchlorinated water
- 1 teaspoon liquid rennet diluted in $\frac{1}{4}$ cup cool nonchlorinated water
- Kosher salt

Directions

a) Heat the milks in a nonreactive 10-quart stockpot set in a 102°F water bath over low heat. Bring the milk to 92°F over 15 minutes. Turn off the heat.

b) Sprinkle the starter and bacteria powder over the milk and let rehydrate for 5 minutes. Mix well using a whisk in an up-and-down motion. Cover and maintain the temperature, allowing the milk to ripen for 45 minutes.

c) Add the calcium chloride and gently whisk in for 1 minute. Add the rennet and gently whisk in for 1 minute. Cover and let sit, maintaining the temperature at 92°F for 40 to 45 minutes, or until the curds give a clean break.

d) Cut the curds into $\frac{1}{4}$-inch pieces and stir for 20 minutes, then let rest for 5 minutes. Meanwhile, heat 3 cups of water to 140°F. Ladle out enough whey to expose the tops of the curds. Add enough 140°F water (about 1 to 2 cups) to bring the temperature to 100°F. Over low heat, slowly raise the temperature to 108°F over 30 minutes, gently stirring the curds.

e) When the curds reach 108°F, stop stirring and allow them to settle. Hold at this temperature for 20 minutes.

f) Place a strainer over a bowl or bucket large enough to capture the whey. Line it with damp cheesecloth and gently ladle the curds into it. Let drain for 5 minutes, then transfer the curds, cloth and all, to an 8-inch tomme mold.

g) Pull the cheesecloth up around the curds, tight and smooth. Fold the cloth tails over the curds and set the follower on top. Press at 10 pounds for 30 minutes. Remove the cheese from the mold, unwrap the cheesecloth, tip the cheese over, redress, then press at 15 pounds for 8 hours or overnight.

h) Meanwhile, make a near-saturated brine solution in a noncorrosive container with lid and chill at 50°F to 55°F.

i) Remove the cheese from the mold and cloth. Place it in the brine, cover, and soak at 50°F to 55°F for 12 hours, tipping over once. Remove from the brine and pat dry.

j) Place on a drying rack, cover loosely with cheesecloth, and air-dry at room temperature for 2 days, or until the surface is dry to the touch. tip the cheese over at least two times during this time to even out the drying.

k) Coat with 2 to 3 layers of cheese wax.

l) Place the waxed cheese in an open ripening box or on a shelf to ripen at 50°F and 85 percent humidity for 2 weeks, tipping daily. After 2 weeks, continue the ripening at the warmer temperature of 65°F and 80 percent humidity for 4 to 6 weeks. The cheese may be consumed at this point or moved to the refrigerator to age for another 3 to 4 months.

52. Saffron-infused manchego

MAKES 2 pounds

Ingredients

- $\frac{1}{8}$ teaspoon saffron threads
- 2 gallons pasteurized whole cow's milk
- 1 teaspoon MM 100 powdered mesophilic starter culture
- 1 teaspoon Thermo B powdered thermophilic starter culture
- 1 teaspoon mild lipase powder diluted in $\frac{1}{4}$ cup cool nonchlorinated water
- 1 teaspoon calcium chloride diluted in $\frac{1}{4}$ cool nonchlorinated water
- 1 teaspoon liquid rennet diluted in $\frac{1}{4}$ cup cool nonchlorinated water
- 1 teaspoon sweet paprika
- 1 cup olive oil

Directions

a) In a nonreactive 10-quart stockpot, stir the saDron into the milk, then heat over low heat to 86°F; this should take about 15 minutes. Turn off the heat.

b) Sprinkle the starter cultures over the milk and let rehydrate for 5 minutes.

c) Mix well using a whisk in an up-and-down motion. Cover and maintain 86°F, allowing the milk to ripen for 45 minutes. Add the lipase, if using (it lends a stronger flavor and aroma), gently whisking it in.

d) Add the calcium chloride and gently whisk in, then add the rennet and gently whisk in for 1 minute. Cover and let sit, maintaining 86°F for 30 to 45 minutes, or until the curds give a clean break.

e) Still maintaining 86°F, cut the curds into $\frac{1}{2}$-inch pieces and let sit for 5 minutes. Cut the curds into rice-size pieces by gently stirring them with a stainless steel whisk. Switching to a rubber spatula, slowly stir around the edges of the pot, keeping the curds moving for about 30 minutes to release the whey and firm up the curds.

f) Over low heat, bring the curds to 104°F over 30 minutes, gently stirring with a rubber spatula to prevent the curds from matting into one mass. The whey will be a light greenish yellow color and only slightly cloudy.

g) Turn off the heat when the temperature reaches 104°F and let the curds rest for 5 minutes. The curds will sink to the bottom. Ladle enough whey to expose the curds.

h) Place a strainer over a bowl or bucket large enough to capture the whey. Line it with damp butter muslin and gently ladle the curds into it. Let drain for 15 minutes, or until the whey stops dripping.

i) Gently transfer the sack of drained curds to an 8-inch tomme mold. Pull the cloth up tight and smooth around the curds, cover with the tails of cloth, and place the follower on top. Press at 15 pounds for 15 minutes.

j) Remove the cheese from the mold, unwrap the cloth, tip the cheese over, and redress. Press again at 15 pounds for 15 minutes. Repeat this process one more time, then tip and redress the cheese and press at 30 pounds for 8 hours or overnight.

k) Make 3 quarts of medium-saturated brine in a noncorrosive container with a lid and chill to 50°F to 55°F. Remove the cheese from the mold and cloth. Place it in the brine and soak at 50°F to 55°F for 6 to 8 hours. Remove the cheese from the brine and pat dry.

l) Place the cheese on a drying mat in an uncovered ripening box and age at 55°F and 80 to 85 percent humidity for 10 days to 3 months, tipping daily. Remove any unwanted mold with cheesecloth dampened in a vinegar-salt solution.

m) When the cheese has reached the desired ripeness, combine the paprika and olive oil and rub the cheese with this mixture. Wrap and store in the refrigerator.

53. Parmesan

MAKES 1¾ pounds

Ingredients

- 2 gallons pasteurized reduced fat (2 percent) cow's milk
- ¼ teaspoon Thermo B powdered thermophilic starter culture
- 1 teaspoon calcium chloride diluted in ¼ cup cool nonchlorinated water
- 1 teaspoon liquid rennet diluted in ¼ cup cool nonchlorinated water Kosher Salt Olive oil for rubbing

Directions

a) Heat the milk in a nonreactive 10-quart stockpot set in a 104°F water bath over low heat. Bring the milk to 94°F over 20 minutes. Turn off the heat.

b) Sprinkle the starter over the milk and let it rehydrate for 5 minutes. Mix well using a whisk in an up-and-down motion. Cover and maintain the temperature, letting the milk ripen for 45 minutes.

Add the calcium chloride and gently whisk in for 1 minute. Add the rennet and gently whisk in for 1 minute. Cover and let sit, maintaining 94°F for 45 minutes, or until the curds give a clean break.

c) Using a whisk, cut the curds into pea-size pieces and let sit undisturbed for 10 minutes. Over low heat, slowly raise the temperature to 124°F over 1 hour, continuously stirring the curds to Firm them up. Once 124°F has been reached, stop stirring and allow the curds to settle and mat together. Cover and maintain 124°F for 10 minutes.

d) Line a colander with damp butter muslin and ladle the curds into it. Let drain for 5 minutes, then transfer the curds, cloth and all, to a 5-inch tomme mold and let drain for minutes.

e) Pull up the cloth and smooth out any wrinkles, fold the tails of the cloth over the curds, and put the follower on top. Press at 10 pounds for 30 minutes. Remove the cheese from the mold, tip it over, and redress, then press again at 10 pounds for 1 hour. Once again remove from the mold, Hip, and redress the cheese, then press at 20 pounds for 12 hours.

f) Make 2 quarts of near-saturated brine and chill to 50°F to 55°F. Remove the cheese from the mold and cloth and place in the brine to soak at 50°F to 55°F for 12 hours, tipping it over once during that time.

g) Remove the cheese from the brine and pat dry. Place on a drying rack, cover with cheesecloth, and air-dry at room temperature for 2 to 3 days, or until the surface is dry to the touch, tipping each day.

h) Place on a mat in a ripening box and ripen at 50°F to 55°F and 85 percent humidity, tipping daily, for 2 weeks. Flip twice a week for the next month, then once a week for the duration of ripening. Remove any unwanted mold with cheesecloth dampened in a vinegar-salt solution.

i) After 3 months of ripening, rub the surface with olive oil. Return the cheese to the ripening box and age for a total of 7 months, or until the desired ripeness is reached, tipping once a week and rubbing with olive oil once a month. Wrap and store in the refrigerator.

54. Romano

MAKES 2 pounds

Ingredients

- 1 gallon pasteurized whole cow's milk
- 1 gallon pasteurized goat's milk
- $\frac{1}{4}$ teaspoon Thermo B powdered thermophilic starter culture
- 1 teaspoon Capalase lipase powder dissolved in $\frac{1}{4}$ cup cool nonchlorinated water before using
- 1 teaspoon calcium chloride diluted in $\frac{1}{4}$ cup cool nonchlorinated water
- 1 teaspoon liquid rennet diluted in $\frac{1}{4}$ cup cool nonchlorinated water Kosher Salt Olive oil for rubbing

Directions

a) Heat the milks in a nonreactive 10-quart stockpot set in a 100°F water bath over low heat. Bring the milk to 90°F over 20 minutes. Turn off the heat.

b) Sprinkle the starter over the milk and let it rehydrate for 5 minutes. Mix well using a whisk in an up-and-down motion. Cover and maintain 90°F, letting the milk ripen for 30 minutes.

c) Add the lipase, if using, and gently whisk in. Add the calcium chloride and gently whisk in for 1 minute. Add the rennet and gently whisk in for 1 minute. Cover and let sit, maintaining 90°F for 1 hour, or until the curds give a clean break.

d) Cut the curds into $\frac{1}{4}$-inch pieces and let sit undisturbed for 5 minutes. Over low heat, slowly raise the temperature to 117°F over 40 to 50 minutes, continuously stirring the curds to firm them up. Once 117°F has been reached, stop stirring and allow the curds to settle. Cover and maintain 117°F for 30 minutes.

e) Line a colander with damp butter muslin and ladle the curds into it. Let drain for 5 minutes, then transfer the curds, cloth and all, to a 5-inch tomme mold. Pull up the cloth and smooth out any wrinkles, fold the tails of the cloth over the curds, and put the follower on top.

Press at 10 pounds for 30 minutes. Remove the cheese from the mold, tip it over, and redress, then press again at 10 pounds for 1 hour. Once again remove, tip, and redress the cheese, then press at 20 pounds for 12 hours.

f) Make 2 quarts of near-saturated brine and chill to 50°F to 55°F. Remove the cheese from the mold and cloth and place in the brine to soak at 50°F to 55°F for 12 hours, tipping it over once during that time.

g) Remove the cheese from the brine and pat dry. Place on a drying rack, cover with cheesecloth, and air-dry at room temperature for 2 days, or until the surface is dry to the touch, tipping each day.

h) Place the cheese on a cheese mat in a ripening box and ripen at 50°F to 55°F and 85 percent humidity, tipping daily for 2 weeks. Flip twice a week for the next month, then once a week for the duration of ripening. Remove any unwanted mold with cheesecloth dampened in a vinegar-salt solution.

i) After 2 months of ripening, rub the surface with olive oil. Return the cheese to the ripening box and age for a total of 5 months, or until the desired ripeness is reached, tipping once a week and rubbing with olive oil once a month. Wrap and store in the refrigerator.

55.   Asiago pepato

MAKES Two 1-pound wheels

Ingredients

- 6 quarts pasteurized whole cow's milk
- 2 quarts pasteurized reduced fat (2 percent) cow's milk
- 1 teaspoon Thermo B powdered thermophilic starter culture
- 1 teaspoon calcium chloride diluted in $\frac{1}{4}$ cup cool nonchlorinated water
- 1 teaspoon liquid rennet diluted in $\frac{1}{4}$ cup cool nonchlorinated water
- $1\frac{1}{2}$ teaspoons black or green peppercorns
- Kosher salt

Directions

a) In a nonreactive 10-quart stockpot, heat the milks over low heat to 92°F; this should take about 20 minutes.

b) Sprinkle the starter over the milk and let it rehydrate for 5 minutes. Mix well using a whisk in an up-and-down motion.

Cover and maintain 92°F, allowing the milk to ripen for minutes.

c) Add the calcium chloride and gently whisk in for 1 minute. Add the rennet and gently whisk in for 1 minute. Cover and let sit, maintaining 92°F for 1 hour, or until the curds give a clean break.

d) Cut the curds into ½-inch pieces and let sit undisturbed for 5 minutes. Over low heat, slowly raise the temperature to 104°F over 40 minutes. Remove from the heat and stir for few minutes to release whey and shrink the curds to the size of peanuts.

e) Over low heat, slowly raise the temperature to 118°F, stirring the curds to firm them up. Once 118°F has been reached, stop stirring and allow the curds to settle. Cover and maintain 118°F for 20 minutes.

f) Ladle enough whey to expose the curds. Line two 4⅝-inch-wide Italian draining baskets with damp cheesecloth and place them on a draining rack. Fill each mold with one-fourth of the curds and let drain for 5 minutes.

g) Cover with the tails of the cheesecloth and gently press with your hand to compact the curds. Unwrap and sprinkle half of the peppercorns over each mold of compacted curds. Divide the remaining curds between the molds to cover the peppercorns and pack down using your hand.

h) Pull the cheesecloth up around the curds and fold it over to cover the tops. Place a follower on top of each draining basket and press at 8 pounds for 1 hour. Remove, tip, and redress the cheese, then press at 8 pounds for another 8 hours.

i) Make 3 quarts of saturated brine and chill to 50°F to 55°F. Remove the cheeses from the molds and cloth and place them in the brine to soak at 50°F to 55°F for 12 hours, tipping them over once.

j) Remove the cheeses from the brine and pat dry. Place on a drying rack, cover loosely with cheesecloth, and air-dry at room temperature for 8 hours, or until the surface is dry to the touch, tipping the cheeses at least one time during the drying process.

k) Place the cheeses on a mat in a ripening box with a lid. Cover loosely and ripen at 54°F and 85 percent humidity, tipping daily for 1 week. Brush with a simple brine, cooled to 50°F to 55°F, twice a week for the rest 3 weeks of aging.

l) For an aged version, continue the brushing process once a week for at least 2 months and up to 1 year.

56. American brick

MAKES 2 pounds

Ingredients

- 2 gallons pasteurized whole cow's milk
- 1 teaspoon Meso II powdered mesophilic starter culture
- 1 teaspoon calcium chloride diluted in $\frac{1}{4}$ cup cool nonchlorinated water
- 1 teaspoon liquid rennet diluted in $\frac{1}{4}$ cup cool nonchlorinated water
- Kosher salt

Directions

a) In a nonreactive 10-quart stockpot, heat the milk over low heat to 88°F; this should take about 20 minutes.

b) Sprinkle the starter over the milk and let it rehydrate for 5 minutes. Mix well using a whisk in an up-and-down motion. Cover and maintain 88°F, letting the milk ripen for 15 minutes. Add the calcium chloride and gently whisk in for 1 minute. Add the rennet and gently whisk in for 1 minute. Cover and let sit, maintaining 88°F for 30 to 45 minutes, or until the curds give a clean break.

c) Still maintaining 88°F, cut the curds into $\frac{1}{2}$-inch pieces and let sit for 5 minutes. Over low heat, slowly bring the curds to 98°F over 45 minutes. Stir continuously to keep the curds from matting together; they will release whey, Firm up slightly, and shrink to the size of peanuts.

d) Once the curds are at 98°F, turn off the heat, maintain the temperature, and let the curds rest undisturbed for 25 minutes; they will sink to the bottom.

e) Line a strainer with damp butter muslin and ladle the curds into it. Let drain for 5 minutes, then transfer the curds, cloth and all, to an 8-inch tomme mold.

f) Pull up the cloth and smooth out any wrinkles, cover the curds with the tails of cloth, set the follower on top, and press at 5 pounds for 15 minutes. Remove the cheese, unwrap, tip, and redress, then press again at 10 pounds for 12 hours.

g) Make 3 quarts of near-saturated brine and chill to 50°F to 55°F. Remove the cheese from the mold and cloth and place it in the brine to soak at 50°F to 55°F for 2 hours.

h) Remove the cheese from the brine and pat dry. Air-dry on a cheese mat at room temperature for about 24 hours to dry and set up the rind. Rub o any mold spots that might develop with a solution of salt and distilled vinegar.

i) Wax the cheese and age at 50°F and 85 percent humidity for up to 4 months, tipping the cheese once a week for even ripening.

57. Caerphilly

MAKES 2 pounds

Ingredients

- 2 gallons pasteurized whole cow's milk
- 1 teaspoon MA 4001 powdered mesophilic starter culture
- 1 teaspoon Aroma B powdered mesophilic starter culture
- 1 teaspoon calcium chloride diluted in $\frac{1}{4}$ cup cool nonchlorinated water
- 1 teaspoon liquid rennet diluted in $\frac{1}{4}$ cup cool nonchlorinated water Kosher salt

Directions

a) In a nonreactive 10-quart stockpot, heat the milk over low heat to 90°F; this should take about 20 minutes.

b) Sprinkle the starter cultures over the milk and let rehydrate for 5 minutes. Mix well using a whisk in an up-and-down motion. Cover and maintain 90°F, letting the milk ripen for 1 hour. Add the calcium chloride and gently whisk in for 1 minute. Add the rennet and gently whisk in for 1 minute.

c) Cover and let sit, maintaining 90°F for 45 to 55 minutes, or until the curds give a clean break.

d) Still maintaining 90°F, cut the curds into ½-inch pieces and let sit for 5 minutes. Over low heat, slowly bring the curds to 95°F over 20 minutes. Stir continuously to keep the curds from matting together; they will release whey, Firm up slightly, and shrink to the size of peanuts.

e) Once the curds are at 95°F, turn off the heat, maintain the temperature, and let the curds rest undisturbed for 45 minutes; they will sink to the bottom.

f) Ladle enough whey from the pot to expose the tops of the curds. Line a strainer with damp butter muslin and ladle the curds into it. Let drain for 5 minutes.

g) Transfer the curds, cloth and all, to an 8-inch tomme mold. Pull up the cloth and smooth out any wrinkles, cover the curds with the tails of cloth, set the follower on top, and press at 8 pounds for 30 minutes. Remove the cheese from the mold, unwrap, Hip, and redress, then press again at 10 pounds for 12 hours.

h) Make 3 quarts of medium-heavy brine and chill to 50°F to 55°F. Remove the cheese from the mold and cloth and place it in the brine to soak at 50°F to 55°F for 8 hours.

i) Remove the cheese from the brine and pat dry. Air-dry on a cheese mat at room temperature for about 24 hours, or until the surface is dry to the touch. Rub any mold spots that might develop with a solution of salt and distilled vinegar.

j) Place the cheese on a mat in a ripening box and ripen at 50°F to 55°F and 85 percent humidity, tipping daily. After 10 to 14 days a whitish gray mold will appear. Once this occurs, tip the cheese twice a week until a crust is formed. Brush the surface twice a week at the same time as you Pip the cheese to encourage mold growth.

k) Brush with a wad of dry cheesecloth or a dedicated soft nailbrush dampened in simple brine with the excess moisture removed. After 3 weeks from the beginning of ripening, the cheese will begin to soften under the crust.

58. Colby

MAKES 2 pounds

Ingredients

- 2 gallons pasteurized whole cow's milk
- $\frac{1}{2}$ teaspoon Meso II powdered mesophilic starter culture
- 1 teaspoon liquid annatto diluted in $\frac{1}{4}$ cup cool nonchlorinated water
- $\frac{1}{2}$ teaspoon calcium chloride diluted in $\frac{1}{4}$ cup cool nonchlorinated water
- $\frac{1}{2}$ teaspoon liquid rennet diluted in $\frac{1}{4}$ cup cool nonchlorinated water
- Kosher salt

Directions

a) In a nonreactive 10-quart stockpot, heat the milk over low heat to 86°F; this should take about 15 minutes.

b) Sprinkle the starter over the milk and let it rehydrate for 5 minutes. Mix well using a whisk in an up-and-down motion.

c) Cover and maintain 86°F, letting the milk ripen for 1 hour. Add the annatto and

gently whisk in for 1 minute. Add the
calcium chloride and gently whisk in for 1
minute, and then incorporate the rennet
in the same way. Cover and let sit,
maintaining 86°F for 30 to 45 minutes,
or until the curds give a clean break.

d) Still maintaining 86°F, cut the curds into
$\frac{1}{2}$-inch pieces and let sit for 5 minutes.
Over low heat, slowly bring the curds to
104°F over 50 minutes. Stir continuously
to keep the curds from matting together;
they will release whey, Firm up slightly,
and shrink to the size of peanuts.

e) Once the curds are at 104°F, turn off
the heat, maintain the temperature, and
let the curds rest undisturbed for 15
minutes; they will sink to the bottom.

f) Into a measuring cup, ladle out enough
whey to expose the curds. Replace the
whey with the same amount of 104°F
water. Gently stir for 2 minutes, then
cover and let the curds rest for 10
minutes.

g) Line a strainer with damp butter muslin and ladle the curds into it. Let drain for 5 minutes.

h) Line a 5-inch tomme mold with damp cheesecloth and gently transfer the drained curds to the mold.

i) Pull up the cloth and smooth out any wrinkles, cover the curds with the cloth tails, set the follower on top, and press at 5 pounds for 1 hour. Remove the cheese from the mold, unwrap, tip, and redress, then press again at 10 pounds for 12 hours.

j) Make 4 quarts of medium-heavy brine and chill to 50°F to 55°F. Remove the cheese from the mold and cloth and place it in the brine to soak at 50°F to 55°F for 8 hours.

k) Remove the cheese from the brine and pat dry. Air-dry at room temperature on a cheese mat for about 24 hours, or until the surface is dry to the touch. Rub o any mold spots that might develop with a solution of salt and distilled vinegar.

l) Wax the cheese and age at 50°F and 80 to 85 percent humidity for 6 weeks to 2 months, tipping the cheese once a week for even ripening.

59. Brew-curds cheddar

MAKES 2 pounds

Ingredients

- 2 gallons pasteurized whole cow's milk
- ½ teaspoon Meso II powdered mesophilic starter culture
- 1 teaspoon liquid annatto diluted in ¼ cup cool nonchlorinated water
- ½ teaspoon calcium chloride diluted in ¼ cup cool nonchlorinated water
- ½ teaspoon liquid rennet diluted in ¼ cup cool nonchlorinated water
- One 12-ounce bottle dark ale or stout at room temperature
- 1 tablespoon kosher salt

Directions

a) Heat the milk in a nonreactive 10-quart stockpot set in a 98°F water bath over low heat. Bring the milk to 88°F over 10 minutes. Turn off the heat.

b) Sprinkle the starter over the milk and let it rehydrate for 5 minutes. Mix well using a whisk in an up-and-down motion. Cover and maintain 88°F, letting the milk ripen for 45 minutes. Add the annatto, if using, and gently whisk in for 1 minute. Add the calcium chloride and gently whisk in for 1 minute, and then incorporate the rennet in the same way. Cover and let sit, maintaining 88°F for 30 to 45 minutes, or until the curds give a clean break.

c) Still maintaining 88°F, cut the curds into $\frac{1}{2}$-inch pieces and let sit for 5 minutes. Over low heat, slowly bring the curds to 102°F over 40 minutes. Stir continuously to keep the curds from matting together; they will release whey, Firm up slightly, and shrink to the size of peanuts.

d) Once the curds are at 102°F, turn off the heat, maintain the temperature, and let the curds rest undisturbed for 30 minutes; they will sink to the bottom.

e) Place a strainer over a bowl or bucket large enough to capture the whey. Line it with damp butter muslin and ladle the curds into it. Let drain for 10 minutes, or until the whey stops tipping. Reserve one-third of the whey and return it to the pot.

f) Return the whey in the pot to 102°F. Place the curds in a colander, set the colander over the pot, and cover. Carefully maintaining the 102°F temperature of the whey, wait minutes for the curds to melt into a slab.

g) Flip the slab of curds, and repeat every 15 minutes for 1 hour. The curds should maintain a 95°F to 100°F temperature from the heated whey below and continue to expel whey into the pot. After 1 hour, the curds will look shiny and white, like poached chicken.

h) Transfer the warm slab of curds to a cutting board and cut into 2 by $\frac{1}{2}$-inch strips, like French fries. Place the warm strips in a bowl and cover completely with the brew. Soak for 45 minutes. Drain and discard the brew. Sprinkle the salt over the curds and gently toss to mix.

i) Line a 5-inch tomme mold with damp cheesecloth. Pack the drained curds into the mold, cover with the cloth tails, set the follower on top, and press at 8 pounds for 1 hour. Remove the cheese from the mold, unwrap, Rip, and redress, then press at 10 pounds for hours.

j) Remove the cheese from the mold and cloth and pat dry. Air-dry on a cheese mat at room temperature for 1 to 2 days, or until the surface is dry to the touch.

k) Wax the cheese and ripen at 50°F to 55°F and 85 percent humidity for 4 to 6 weeks, tipping the cheese daily for even ripening.

60.   Cheddar-Jalapeño Cheese Curds

MAKES 1 pound

Ingredients

- 1 gallon pasteurized whole cow's milk
- $\frac{1}{8}$ teaspoon Meso II powdered mesophilic starter culture
- 1 teaspoon calcium chloride diluted in 2 tablespoons cool nonchlorinated water
- 1 teaspoon liquid rennet diluted in 2 tablespoons cool nonchlorinated water
- 1 tablespoon plus $\frac{1}{2}$ teaspoon kosher salt
- 1 (4-ounce) can diced jalapeños, drained
- $\frac{1}{2}$ to 1 teaspoon red pepper Rakes

Directions

a) Heat the milk in a nonreactive 6-quart stockpot set in a 98°F water bath over low heat.

b) Bring the milk to 88°F over 12 minutes. Turn off the heat.

c) Sprinkle the starter over the milk and let it rehydrate for 5 minutes. Mix well using a whisk in an up-and-down motion. Cover and maintain 88°F, letting the milk ripen for 45 minutes. Add the calcium chloride and gently whisk in. Add the rennet and gently whisk in. Cover and let sit, maintaining 86°F to 88°F for 40 minutes, or until the curds give a clean break.

d) Cut the curds into ½-inch pieces and let them rest for 5 minutes. Over low heat, slowly bring the curds to 102°F over about 30 minutes, stirring to reduce the curds to the size of peanuts. Turn off the heat and maintain 102°F for 30 minutes, stirring every couple of minutes to prevent matting.

e) Give the curds a texture test: squeeze a spoonful of curds; they should lump together. Now push them apart with your thumb; if they separate, you are ready to proceed. Let the curds settle for 15 minutes.

f) Place a strainer over a bowl or bucket large enough to capture the whey. Line it with damp butter muslin and ladle the curds into it. Let drain for 10 minutes, or until the whey stops tipping. Pour the whey back into the pot.

g) Return the whey in the pot to 102°F. Place the curds in a colander, set the colander over the pot, and cover.

h) Carefully maintaining the 102°F temperature of the whey, wait a few minutes for the curds to melt into a slab. Flip the slab of curds, and repeat every 15 minutes for 1 hour. The curds should maintain a 98°F to 100°F temperature from the heated whey below and continue to expel whey into the pot. After 1 hour, the curds will look shiny and white, like poached chicken.

i) Transfer the warm slab of curds to a cutting board and cut into 2 by ½-inch strips, like French fries. Place the warm strips in a bowl, add the 1 tablespoon of salt, and mix with your hands. Put the salted curds in a strainer over a bowl to dry, uncovered, for 12 to 24 hours at room temperature.

j) Place the curds in a large bowl. Gently mix in the ½ teaspoon of salt, the jalapeños, and the red pepper Hakes. Store the curds in a resealable bag or vacuum-seal and refrigerate. They'll keep for 1 to 2 weeks in the refrigerator.

61. Sharp cheddar

Ingredients

- 1 cup raw cashews
- 1/4 cup refined coconut oil, plus more for greasing the pan
- 1 cup raw almonds
- 1 cup filtered water
- 1/4 cup modified tapioca starch
- Beta-carotene from 3 beta-carotene gel caps, squeezed out of the gel caps 1 teaspoon Himalayan salt
- $2\frac{1}{2}$ tablespoons agar-agar flakes
- 1 tablespoon apple cider vinegar

Directions:

a) Place the cashews in filtered water in a small bowl. Cover and refrigerate overnight.

b) Lightly oil a 4-inch spring form pan with coconut oil.

c) Bring 4 cups water to a boil in a medium saucepan over medium-high heat. Add the almonds and blanch them for 1 minute.

267

Drain the almonds in a colander and
remove the skins with your fingers (you
can compost the skins).

d) Drain the cashews. In the pitcher of a
Blender, place the cashews, almonds,
water, modified tapioca starch, beta-
carotene, coconut oil, salt, and agar-agar.

e) Blend on high speed for 1 minute or until
smooth.

f) Transfer the mixture to a small saucepan
and heat over medium-low heat, stirring
continuously, until it becomes thick and
cheese-like in consistency.

g) Fold in the vinegar.

h) Pour the cheese into the prepared spring
form pan. Let it cool, then place it in the
fridge overnight to set up.

i) Run a sharp knife around the inside edge
of the pan. Release the buckle and
remove the ring of the mold. Using the
flat edge of a large knife, separate the
cheese from the bottom metal round and
transfer to a cutting board. With a very
sharp knife, slice the cheese and serve.

j) If you want to grate this cheese, turn it out of the mold and place it in a humidifier or wine cooler at 54 degrees F for 1 to 3 weeks. Salt your cheese every few days to prevent black mold from forming.

k) When you feel your cheese is aged sufficiently, cut the round in 8 small wedges, place in plastic wrap, and transfer to the refrigerator for 24 hours.

l) Grate the small cheese wedges on a large grater.

62.   Farmhouse Chive Cheddar

MAKES 2 pounds

Ingredients

- 2 gallons pasteurized whole cow's milk
- $\frac{1}{2}$ teaspoon Meso II powdered mesophilic starter culture
- 1 teaspoon liquid annatto diluted in $\frac{1}{4}$ cup cool nonchlorinated water
- $\frac{1}{2}$ teaspoon calcium chloride diluted in $\frac{1}{4}$ cup cool nonchlorinated water
- $\frac{1}{2}$ teaspoon liquid rennet diluted in $\frac{1}{4}$ cup cool nonchlorinated water
- Kosher salt
- 2 teaspoons dried chives

Directions

a) Heat the milk in a nonreactive 10-quart stockpot set in a 96°F water bath over low heat. Bring the milk to 86°F over 10 minutes. Turn off the heat.

b) Sprinkle the starter over the milk and let it rehydrate for 5 minutes. Mix well using a whisk in an up-and-down motion. Cover and maintain 86°F, letting the milk ripen for 1 hour. Add the annatto and gently whisk in for 1 minute. Add the calcium chloride and gently whisk in for 1 minute, and then incorporate the rennet in the same way. Cover and let sit, maintaining 86°F for 30 to 45 minutes, or until the curds give a clean break.

c) Still maintaining 86°F, cut the curds into ½-inch pieces and let sit for 5 minutes. Over low heat, slowly bring the curds to 102°F over 40 minutes.

d) Turn off the heat, maintain temperature, and gently stir the curds for 20 minutes, or until they start to firm up. The curds will be the size of peanuts. Still maintaining 104°F, let the curds rest undisturbed for 30 minutes; they will sink to the bottom.

e) Ladle enough whey to expose the top of the curds. Stir continuously for 15 to 20 minutes, or until the curds are matted and cling together when pressed in your hand.

f) Line a strainer with damp butter muslin and ladle the curds into it. Let drain for

5 minutes, then toss in 2 teaspoons of salt and the chives and mix thoroughly with your hands.

g) Line an 8-inch tomme mold with damp cheesecloth and gently transfer the drained curds to the lined mold. Pull up the cloth and smooth out any wrinkles, cover the curds with the cloth tails, set the follower on top, and press at 8 pounds for 1 hour.

h) Remove the cheese from the mold, unwrap, tip, and redress, and press at 10 pounds for 12 hours.

i) Make 3 quarts of near-saturated brine and chill to 50°F to 55°F. Remove the cheese from the mold and cheesecloth and place in the brine to soak at 50°F to 55°F for 8 hours.

j) Remove the cheese from the brine and pat dry. Air-dry on a cheese mat at room temperature for about 24 hours, until the surface is dry to the touch.

k) Rub out any mold spots that might develop with a solution of salt and distilled vinegar.

l) Wax the cheese and age at 50°F and 80 to 85 percent humidity for 1 to 2 months, tipping the cheese once a week for even ripening.

63. Irish-style cheddar

MAKES 2 pounds

Ingredients

- 2 gallons pasteurized whole cow's milk
- 1 teaspoon MA 4001 powdered mesophilic starter culture
- 1 teaspoon calcium chloride diluted in $\frac{1}{4}$ cup cool nonchlorinated water
- 1 teaspoon liquid rennet diluted in $\frac{1}{4}$ cup cool nonchlorinated water
- 2 cups Irish whiskey at room temperature
- 1 tablespoon kosher salt

Directions

a) Heat the milk in a nonreactive 10-quart stockpot set in a 98°F water bath over low heat. Bring the milk to 88°F over 10 minutes. Turn off the heat.

b) Sprinkle the starter over the milk and let it rehydrate for 5 minutes. Mix well using a whisk in an up-and-down motion. Cover and maintain 88°F, letting the milk ripen for 45 minutes. Add the calcium chloride and gently whisk in for 1 minute. Add the rennet and gently whisk in for 1 minute. Cover and let sit, maintaining 88°F for 30 to 45 minutes, or until the curds give a clean break.

c) Still maintaining 88°F, cut the curds into $\frac{1}{2}$-inch pieces and let sit for 5 minutes. Over low heat, slowly bring the curds to 102°F over 40 minutes. Stir continuously to keep the curds from matting together; they will release whey, Firm up slightly, and shrink to the size of peanuts.

d) Once the curds are at 102°F, turn off the heat, maintain the temperature, and let the curds rest undisturbed for 30 minutes; they will sink to the bottom.

e) Place a strainer over a bowl or bucket large enough to capture the whey. Line it with damp butter muslin and ladle the curds into it. Let drain for 15 minutes, or until the whey stops dripping. Pour the whey back into the pot.

f) Return the whey in the pot to 102°F. Place the curds in a colander, set the colander over the pot, and cover. Carefully maintaining the 102°F temperature of the whey, wait some minutes for the curds to melt into a slab. Flip the slab of curds, and repeat every 15 minutes for 1 hour.

g) The curds should maintain a 95°F to 100°F temperature from the heated whey below and will continue to expel whey into the pot. After an hour, the curds will look shiny and white, like poached chicken.

h) Transfer the warm slab of curds to a cutting board and cut into 2 by $\frac{1}{2}$-inch strips, like French fries. Place the warm strips in a bowl and add $\frac{1}{4}$ cup of the whiskey and the salt. Gently toss with your hands to combine.

i) Line an 8-inch tomme mold with damp cheesecloth. Pack the drained curds into the mold, cover with the cloth tails, set the follower on top, and press at 10 pounds for 1 hour. Remove the cheese from the mold, unwrap, tip, and redress, then press at 15 pounds for 12 hours.

j) Remove the cheese from the mold and cloth, place in a container, and cover with the remaining 1¾ cups of whiskey. Cover the container and place it in a 55°F environment for 8 hours, tipping the cheese once during that time.

k) Drain the cheese and pat dry. Discard the soaking whiskey. Place the cheese on a cheese mat and air-dry at room temperature for 1 to 2 days, or until the surface is dry to the touch.

l) Wax the cheese and ripen at 50°F to 55°F and 85 percent humidity for 2 to 3 months, tipping the cheese daily during the first week and twice a week thereafter for even ripening.

64. Double-Milled Cheddar

Directions

a) In double-milled cheddars the natural, white cheddar curds are broken or cut up and pressed twice. The cheddar goes through its initial cheddaring process where the curds are broken up before molding and pressing. The curds are then pressed, brined, and aged to a specified desired maturity, and then are broken apart or cut into pieces (milled) a second time.

b) At this point the milled curds are flavored by tossing with any number of sweet or flavoring ingredients or by soaking in alcohol before being molded and pressed again. Once double-milled, the cheddar is further aged to assure that the milled curds bind together to form a cheddar wheel.

c) To make flavored Double-Milled Cheddar: This flavoring process can be applied to good quality store-bought white or orange cheddar.

d) Cut or shred the curds into irregular cubes or pieces of about $\frac{3}{8}$ inch to $\frac{1}{2}$ inch.

Place them in a bowl and add the flavoring, gently but thoroughly mixing with your hands.

e) For herbs or spices, the proportion should be 1-part herb or spice to 6 parts cheese. Fill a cloth-lined cheddar mold or cheese press with the flavored cheese and press following steps 8 to 10 for Brew-Curds Cheddar.

f) To make stout or whisky cheddar, for every one pound of cheese you will use 10 to 12 ounces of brew or spirits, or enough to cover the milled curds.

g) Soak the curds for 4 to 6 hours, then drain and your mold or press. Follow steps 8 to 10 for Brew-Curds Cheddar for pressing and finishing instructions.

h) Then wax and store at 50°F to 55°F and 75 percent humidity or vacuum-seal and refrigerate. Allow the new cheese to age for at least 2 weeks or up to a few months before consuming

COATED AND RUBBED CHEESES

65.   Brin d'Amour

MAKES 1 pound

Ingredients

- 2 quarts pasteurized goat's milk
- 2 quarts pasteurized whole cow's milk
- $\frac{1}{4}$ teaspoon MA 4001 powdered mesophilic starter culture
- 1 teaspoon calcium chloride diluted in $\frac{1}{4}$ cup cool nonchlorinated water
- 1 teaspoon liquid rennet diluted in $\frac{1}{4}$ cup cool nonchlorinated water
- 2 teaspoons sea salt
- $1\frac{1}{2}$ teaspoons dried thyme
- $1\frac{1}{2}$ teaspoons dried oregano
- $1\frac{1}{2}$ teaspoons dried savory
- $1\frac{1}{2}$ teaspoons herbes de Provence
- 3 tablespoons dried rosemary
- 1 teaspoon paprika
- 1 teaspoon whole coriander seeds
- 1 teaspoon whole mixed peppercorns
- 1 teaspoon whole juniper berries
- 2 teaspoons olive oil

Directions

a) In a nonreactive 6-quart stockpot, heat the milks over low heat to 86°F; this should take about 15 minutes. Turn off the heat.

b) Sprinkle the starter over the milk and let it rehydrate for 5 minutes. Mix well using a whisk in an up-and-down motion. Add the calcium chloride and gently whisk in, and then add the rennet in the same way.

c) Cover and maintain 72°F, allowing the milk to ripen for 8 hours, or until the curds form one large mass the consistency of thick yogurt and clear whey is coating around the sides of the pot. Check the curds for a clean break. If the cut edge is clean, the curds are ready.

d) Place a strainer over a bowl or bucket large enough to capture the whey. Line it with damp butter muslin. Gently cut $\frac{1}{2}$-inch-thick slices of the curds using a ladle or skimmer and gently ladle the slices into the strainer. Gently toss the curds with 1 teaspoon of the salt, then tie the muslin into a draining sack and hang to let drain at room temperature for 6 to 10 hours, until the whey stops dripping.

e) The longer the curds drain, the drier the finished cheese will be. Alternatively, you can drain the curds by hanging for 45 minutes, then moving the sack to a 4-inch Camembert mold without a bottom, placed on a draining rack. Drain and ripen in the mold for 6 to 10 hours, tipping the curds once during the draining process and sprinkling the remaining 1 teaspoon salt over the surface of the cheese.

f) If not using the mold for the final shape, transfer the sack to a clean work surface and roll the curds into a ball, then flatten slightly with your hands. Open the sack and sprinkle the remaining 1 teaspoon salt over the cheese and lightly rub it into the surface. Set the cheese on a draining rack at room temperature for 8 hours to allow the salt to be absorbed into the cheese and excess moisture to be released. Continue to air-dry for a total of 24 hours, or until the surface is dry.

g) Combine the herbs and spices in a small bowl. Pat the cheese dry of any moisture, then rub thoroughly with the olive oil. Spread a layer of the herb mixture on a sheet of parchment or waxed paper and roll the cheese in the mixture to coat, then gently press the herbs so they stick to the surface of the cheese. Reserve the unused herbs.

h) Cover the cheese with plastic wrap and place in a ripening box at 50°F to 55°F and 80 to 85 percent humidity for 3 days. Remove the plastic wrap, coat with more herbs if needed, and place in a ripening box at 50°F to 55°F for 27 more days. The cheese will be ready to eat at this point or can be aged for another month.

66. Cocoa-Rubbed Dry Jack Cheese

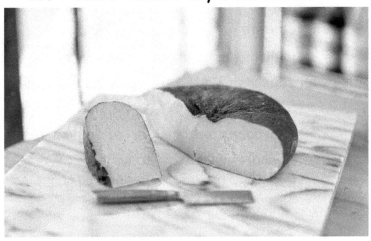

MAKES 2 pounds

Ingredients

- 2 gallons pasteurized whole cow's milk
- 1 teaspoon MA 4001 powdered mesophilic starter culture
- 1 teaspoon calcium chloride diluted in $\frac{1}{4}$ cup cool nonchlorinated water
- 1 teaspoon liquid rennet diluted in $\frac{1}{4}$ cup cool nonchlorinated water
- Kosher salt
- 2 tablespoons cocoa powder
- 2 teaspoons instant espresso
- $1\frac{1}{2}$ teaspoons ground black pepper
- $4\frac{1}{2}$ teaspoons olive oil

Directions

a) In a nonreactive 10-quart stockpot, heat the milk over low heat to 86°F; this should take about 15 minutes.

b) Sprinkle the starter over the milk and let it rehydrate for 5 minutes. Mix well using a whisk in an up-and-down motion. Cover and maintain 86°F, allowing the milk to ripen for 1 hour. Add the calcium chloride and gently whisk in for 1 minute. Add the rennet and gently whisk in for 1 minute. Cover and let sit, maintaining 86°F for 30 to 45 minutes, or until the curds give a clean break.

c) Still maintaining 86°F, cut the curds into $\frac{3}{4}$-inch pieces and let sit for 5 minutes. Over low heat, slowly bring the curds to 102°F over 40 minutes, stirring continuously to keep the curds from matting together. The curds will release whey, firm up slightly, and shrink to the size of dried beans. Maintain 102°F and let the curds rest undisturbed for 30 minutes; they will sink to the bottom.

d) Ladle out enough whey to expose the curds. Still holding the temperature, stir continuously for 15 to 20 minutes, or until the curds are matted and cling together when pressed in your hand.

e) Place a strainer over a bowl or bucket large enough to capture the whey. Line it with damp butter muslin and ladle the curds into it Let drain for 5 minutes, then sprinkle in 1 tablespoon of salt and

gently and thoroughly mix with your
hands.

f) Draw the ends of the cloth together and
    twist to form a ball to help squeeze out
    the excess moisture. Roll the ball on a
    Pat surface to release more whey.

g) Tie the top of the cloth sack, press it
    with your hands to flatten slightly, and
    place it on a cutting board sitting on top
    of a draining rack. Place a second cutting
    board on top of the flattened sack and
    set an 8-pound weight directly over the
    cheese. Press at 75°F to 85°F for 6
    hours for moist Jack or 8 hours for
    drier Jack.

h) Remove the cheese from the sack and
    pat dry. Rub with 1 tablespoon of salt
    and place on a draining rack to air-dry
    for 8 hours.

i) Make 3 quarts of saturated brine and
    chill to 50°F to 55°F. Place the cheese in
    the brine and soak at 50°F to 55°F for 8
    hours, Kipping it over once during that
    time. Remove from the brine, pat dry,
    and air-dry on a rack at room

temperature for hours, or until the surface is dry to the touch. Flip once during this drying period.

j) Place the cheese on a cheese mat in a ripening box at 50°F to 55°F and 85 percent humidity for 1 week, kipping the cheese daily for even ripening.

k) Combine the cocoa, espresso, and pepper in a small bowl. Add the olive oil and stir to combine. Rub one-fourth of the cocoa mixture all over the cheese. Place the cheese on a rack so air circulates all around it, then continue to ripen at 50°F to 55°F overnight. Repeat the rubbing and air-drying process every day for 3 more days, then ripen the cheese at 60°F and 75 percent humidity for 2 months, tipping twice a week.

l) Wrap in cheese paper and refrigerate until ready to eat—up to 10 months or, for a very rich, deep flavor, up to 2 years, if you can wait that long! Once opened, the cheese will dry out and harden as time goes on, creating a wonderful grating cheese.

67. Lavender Mist Chèvre

MAKES Six 4-ounce disks

Ingredients

- 1 gallon pasteurized goat's milk
- $\frac{1}{4}$ teaspoon MA 4001 powdered mesophilic starter culture
- 1 teaspoon calcium chloride diluted in $\frac{1}{4}$ cup cool nonchlorinated water
- 1 teaspoon liquid rennet diluted in $\frac{1}{4}$ cup cool nonchlorinated water
- 1 teaspoon sea salt
- $\frac{1}{2}$ teaspoon fennel pollen powder
- $\frac{1}{4}$ teaspoon ground lavender or lavender buds

Directions

a) In a nonreactive 6-quart stockpot, heat the milk over low heat to 86°F; this should take about 15 minutes. Turn off the heat.

b) Sprinkle the starter over the milk and let it rehydrate for 5 minutes. Mix well using a whisk in an up-and-down motion. Add the calcium chloride and gently whisk in, and then whisk in the rennet in the same way. Cover and maintain 72°F, allowing the milk to ripen for 12 hours, or until the curds have formed one large mass the consistency of thick yogurt and clear whey is coating around the sides of the pot.

c) Place a strainer over a bowl or bucket large enough to capture the whey. Line it with damp butter muslin and gently ladle the curds into the strainer. Add $\frac{1}{2}$ teaspoon of the salt and gently toss to combine. Tie the tails of the cloth to make a draining sack and hang to let drain at room temperature for 6 to 12 hours.

d) Remove the cheese from the cloth and shape it into six 4-ounce round disks. Sprinkle the remaining $\frac{1}{2}$ teaspoon salt over the surface of each cheese and lightly rub it into the surface. Set the cheeses on a drying rack at room temperature for 4 hours to allow them to absorb the salt and release excess moisture.

e) Combine the fennel pollen and lavender in a small bowl. Pat the cheeses dry, then place them on a sheet of parchment or waxed paper and dust all sides with the herb mixture.

f) Place the cheeses on a rack and let sit at room temperature for 1 hour, then wrap each cheese in plastic wrap and refrigerate for at least 3 days to allow the Flavors of the rub to infuse the cheese and up to 10 days.

68. Honey-Rubbed Montasio

MAKES 2 pounds

Ingredients

- 1 gallon pasteurized reduced fat (2 percent) cow's milk
- 1 gallon pasteurized goat's milk
- 1 teaspoon Thermo C powdered thermophilic starter culture
- 1 teaspoon calcium chloride diluted in $\frac{1}{4}$ cup cool nonchlorinated water
- 1 teaspoon liquid rennet diluted in $\frac{1}{4}$ cup cool nonchlorinated water
- 3 teaspoons sea salt
- Kosher salt
- 3 tablespoons honey

Directions

a) In a nonreactive 10-quart pot, heat the milks over low heat to 90°F; this should take about 20 minutes.

b) Sprinkle the starter over the milk and let it rehydrate for 5 minutes. Mix well using a whisk in an up-and-down motion. Cover and maintain 90°F, allowing the milk to ripen for 45 minutes. Add the calcium chloride and gently whisk in for 1 minute. Add the rennet and gently whisk in for 1 minute. Cover and let sit, maintaining 90°F for 30 to 45 minutes, or until the curds give a clean break.

c) Cut the curds into $\frac{1}{2}$-inch pieces and let sit undisturbed for 5 minutes. Over low heat, slowly bring the curds to 104°F over 40 minutes, stirring two or three times. Remove from the heat and stir for 15 minutes to release whey and shrink the curds to the size of peanuts.

d) Over low heat, slowly bring the temperature to 112°F over 5 to 7 minutes, stirring the curds to firm them up. Once 112°F is reached, remove from the heat, maintain the temperature, and let the curds rest for 20 minutes; they will sink to the bottom.

e) Ladle enough whey to expose the curds. Place a strainer over a bowl or bucket large enough to capture the whey. Line it with damp butter muslin and gently ladle the curds into it. Let drain for 10 minutes, then sprinkle $1\frac{1}{2}$ teaspoons of the sea salt over the curds and gently but thoroughly toss with your hands. Let drain for 5 more minutes.

f) Draw the ends of the muslin together to form a ball and twist to help squeeze out the excess moisture. Place the sack on a sanitized cutting board, roll it into a ball, and tie the top to secure the curds in a round shape. Place both wrapped curds and cutting board on a draining rack and press down on the curds with your hands to flatten slightly.

g) Smooth out the knot and ties as best you can to create a stable surface for a second cutting board to rest on. Place the second cutting board on top of the cheese, press down to even out the bundle, then cover the whole assembly completely with a kitchen towel. Place an 8-pound weight over the cheese and press for 8 hours or overnight at 75°F to 85°F.

h) Make 2 quarts of near-saturated brine and chill to 50°F to 55°F. Remove the cheese from the sack and place it in the brine to soak at 50°F to 55°F for 12 hours, tipping it once to brine evenly. Remove the cheese from the brine and pat dry, then place it on a cheese mat or rack to air-dry at room temperature for hours, or until the surface is dry to the touch. Flip once during this time.

i) Place in a ripening box at 50°F to 55°F and 85 percent humidity and age for 1 week, tipping daily. Then brush with a simple brine solution cooled to 50°F to 55°F, twice a week for 2 weeks.

j) After 2 weeks, rub the cheese with $1\frac{1}{2}$ tablespoons of the honey to coat, then return it to the ripening box at 50°F to 55°F and 80 percent humidity for 1 week, tipping daily.

k) After 1 more weeks, rub with the remaining $1\frac{1}{2}$ tablespoons of honey and then with the remaining $1\frac{1}{2}$ teaspoons of salt.

l) Return the cheese to the ripening box for 2 more weeks, tipping daily, then vacuum-seal or wrap tightly in plastic wrap to protect the coating, and store refrigerated for 1 month up to 1 year.

69. Rustico Foglie di Noce

Directions

a) You'll need 4 to 6 large dried walnut leaves, stemmed, blanched, and patted dry.

b) To best emulate the robust flavors that come with the use of sheep's milk, a small amount of cream and a bit of lipase powder are added to the goat's and cow's milks.

c) Make the cheese using the Montasio recipe, combining 1 cup of heavy cream with the milks. After adding the culture and before adding the calcium chloride and rennet, add a pinch of lipase powder.

d) Follow the directions through the first stage of ripening, prior to rubbing with honey (through step 7). Rub the cheese with olive oil, then sprinkle with kosher salt and rub it into the surface. Though it's not traditional, you can rub the cheese with smoked olive oil alternating with unflavored olive oil for a smoky flavor.

e) Brush the walnut leaves on both sides with olive oil, then wrap enough leaves around the cheese to cover it fully. Place the cheese in a ripening box at 50°F to 55°F and 75 percent humidity with good air circulation and age for 3 months, Dipping daily for the first week, then twice a week thereafter.

f) Rub the cheese daily with olive oil. Consume the cheese once it has aged 3 months, or vacuum-seal or wrap in plastic and store refrigerated for another month.

g) When you're ready to serve these cheeses, allow diners to peel away the leaf wrapping on their portion of cheese.

70. Young Époisses

Ingredients

- 500g pack white bread mix
- 100g walnut pieces
- 140g dried apricots, sliced
- 25g poppy seeds, toasted
- 400ml milk
- a little oil, for greasing
- 1 egg, beaten
- 1-2 soft cheeses in boxes, like brie or camembert
- splash of white wine

Directions

a) Tip the bread mix into a food processor, add the walnuts and whizz until fully incorporated. Transfer to a bowl and stir in the apricots and most of the poppy seeds. Warm the milk to hand temperature, then stir into the flour mix with a wooden spoon. Knead in the bowl until smooth. Cover with oiled cling film and leave somewhere warmish to rise for 1 hr.

b) Find a heatproof dish the same size or a bit bigger than your cheese box. Sit it in the middle of a big baking tray.

c) Shape the risen dough into a long, thin log that will wrap around the dish on the sheet, like a wreath. Press the ends together, loosely cover with oiled cling film and leave to rise for 20-30 minutes.

d) Heat oven to 180C/160C fan/gas 4. Brush the egg all over the loaf, then sprinkle with the remaining poppy seeds. Using kitchen scissors, randomly snip into the dough, to give a spiky finish. Bake for 35-40 minutes until golden and crusty, and the bottom sounds hollow when you tap it. Remove the dish from the middle.

e) To serve, unwrap the cheese and put it back into the box. Stab a few times, add the wine and tie kitchen string around the box to secure it in case the glue comes undone. Sit the cheese in the middle of the bread, without its lid, and bake for 10-15 minutes until molten. Serve straight away and, if you like, pop

another cheese in the oven so you can
finish off the bread when the first
cheese box is wiped clean.

BLOOMY-RIND AND SURFACE-RIPENED CHEESES

71. Crème fraîche brie

MAKES One 10- to 12-ounce wheel or two 5- to 6-ounce wheels

Ingredients

- Penicillium candidum mold powder
- Kosher salt
- 2 gallon pasteurized whole cow's milk
- 1 teaspoon Meso II powdered mesophilic starter culture
- 1/8 teaspoon Geotrichum candidum
- 15 mold powder
- 1 teaspoon calcium chloride diluted in $\frac{1}{4}$ cup cool nonchlorinated water
- $\frac{1}{2}$ teaspoon liquid rennet diluted in $\frac{1}{4}$ cup cool nonchlorinated water
- $1\frac{1}{2}$ cups cultured crème fraîche, homemade or store-bought, at room temperature

Directions

a) Twelve hours before starting, combine a pinch of Penicillium candidum, $\frac{1}{4}$ teaspoon salt, and 2 cups of cool nonchlorinated water in an atomizer or spray bottle. Store at 50°F to 55°F.

b) In a nonreactive 6-quart stockpot, slowly heat the milk to 86°F over low heat; this should take about 15 minutes. Turn off the heat.

c) Sprinkle the starter, $\frac{1}{8}$ teaspoon of P. candidum mold powder, and the Geotrichum candidum mold powder over the milk and let rehydrate for 5 minutes. Mix well using a whisk in an up-and-down motion for 20 strokes. Cover and maintain 86°F, letting the milk ripen for 30 minutes. Add the calcium chloride and gently whisk in, then add the rennet in the same way. Cover and let sit, maintaining 86°F for $1\frac{1}{2}$ hours, or until the curds give a clean break.

d) Cut the curds into $\frac{1}{2}$-inch pieces and let sit for 5 minutes to firm up the curds. Using a rubber spatula, gently stir for 5 minutes around the edges of the pot to move the curds around. Let the curds rest for 5 minutes; they will sink to the bottom.

e) Ladle enough whey to expose the curds. Gently ladle the curds into a colander lined with damp butter muslin and let drain for 10 minutes, or until the whey stops dripping.

f) Place the crème fraîche in a bowl and whisk to soften. Using a rubber spatula, gently fold the crème fraîche into the curds to combine. Let drain for 10 minutes, until any residual liquid has drained out.

g) Set a draining rack over a tray, put a cutting board on the rack and a cheese mat on the board, place one 8-inch Brie mold or two 4-inch Camembert molds on the mat. Ladle the curds into the mold or molds and let drain for 2 hours. The curds will reduce to about two-thirds the height of the mold. Place a second mat and board over the top of the mold. With one hand holding the board firmly against the mat and mold, lift and gently flip over the bottom board and mat with the mold and place back onto the draining rack; the second board and mat will now be on the bottom and the original mat and board will be on top.

h) Let drain for 2 hours, until the curds are reduced in size by about one-third, then tip again in the same manner and let drain overnight at room temperature. The curds will be about $1\frac{1}{2}$ inches high at this point.

i) Salt the top of the cheese, tip it over, salt the second side, and let drain for 2 more hours. The quantity of salt is hard to pinpoint, but if you imagine salting a steak or tomato well, that is about right. The curds will be about 1-inch-high at this point. Remove the mold and spray the cheese lightly (while it is on the draining rack) with the P. candidum solution.

j) Place the cheese on a clean cheese mat in a ripening box. Cover loosely with the lid and ripen at 50°F to 55°F and 90 percent humidity. High humidity is essential for making this cheese. Flip the cheese daily, removing any whey that may have accumulated in the ripening box. Keep the box loosely covered to maintain the humidity level.

k) After 2 days, you can lightly spray the cheeses with mold solution again to help ensure proper mold growth, if desired. After about 5 days, the first signs of white fuzzy mold will appear. Remove any undesirable mold with a piece of cheesecloth dipped in a vinegar-salt solution.

l) After 10 to 14 days, the cheeses will be fully coated in white mold. At this point, clean the ripening box, wrap the cheeses in cheese paper, and return them to the ripening box.

m) The cheese will begin to soften within 1 week or so. After a total of 4 weeks from the start of ripening (or 3 weeks if you use Camembert molds), move the wrapped cheeses to the refrigerator and store until they have reached the desired ripeness: firm and mild, or runny and strong.

n) The aging time to desired ripeness will vary depending on the diameter and thickness of the cheese: if a Brie mold was used, count on 4 to 7 weeks total; if 2 Camembert molds, count on 3 to 6 weeks' total.

72. American-style brie

MAKES 2 pounds

Ingredients
- 2 gallons pasteurized whole cow's milk
- $\frac{1}{2}$ cup pasteurized heavy cream
- Pinch of MA 4001 powdered mesophilic starter culture
- 1 teaspoon Thermo B powdered thermophilic starter culture
- 1 teaspoon Penicillium candidum mold powder
- 1 teaspoon Geotrichum candidum 15 mold powder
- 1 teaspoon calcium chloride diluted in $\frac{1}{4}$ cup cool nonchlorinated water
- 1 teaspoon liquid rennet diluted in $\frac{1}{4}$ cup cool nonchlorinated water
- Kosher salt

Directions
a) Heat the milk and cream in a 10-quart stockpot set in a 102°F water bath over low heat. Bring the milk to 90°F over 10 minutes.

b) Leave the heat on and sprinkle the starter cultures and mold powders over the milk and let rehydrate for 5 minutes. Mix well using a whisk in an up-and-down motion for 20 strokes. Allow the temperature of the milk to rise to 96°F to 98°F. Turn off the heat, cover, and let the milk rest in the water bath for $1\frac{1}{2}$ hours. Add the calcium chloride and gently whisk in, then add the rennet in the same way. Let rest, covered, for 30 minutes, or until the curds give a clean break.

c) Cut the curds into $\frac{3}{4}$-inch pieces and let sit for 5 minutes. Stir the curds for 10 to 15 minutes, then let them settle for 5 minutes. Ladle enough whey to expose the curds.

d) Set a draining rack over a tray, put an 8-inch Brie mold (with a bottom) on it, and put the rack in a ripening box. Gently ladle the curds into the mold and let the curds drain for 1 hour, periodically lifting the mold and pouring the whey out of the tray.

e) After 1 hour, gently Rip the cheese out of the mold into your hand, turn it over, and return it to the mold. This evens out the drainage and smoothers the surface on both sides. Flip the cheese every hour as you continue to drain and discard whey. Gradually there will only be a few ounces of whey to drain. When there is no more whey, put a foil cover or lid on the ripening box, vented in two places, and keep the box at room temperature for 8 hours.

f) Drain the last of the whey and unmold the cheese onto a mat. Salt the top of the cheese, tip it over, and salt the second side. The quantity of salt is hard to pinpoint, but if you imagine salting a steak or tomato well, that is about right.

g) The blooming phase of ripening begins now and is best carried out at 52°F to 56°F. Put the lid of the ripening box on askew or cover the middle two-thirds of the pan with aluminum foil, leaving it open at both ends for air circulation. In 3 to 4 days the cheese will bloom, with white mold forming over the surface. Flip the wheel over to bloom the other side. The second bloom will be complete in only 1 or 2 more days.

h) Using cheese paper, wrap the wheel, taping closed any awkward edges. Move the wheel to a clean tray and ripening box with a closed lid. Place 2 wadded damp paper towels at opposite corners of the box to keep the humidity at about 85 percent. Move this box to your refrigerator (set at about 38°F). Moisten the towels as needed and turn the wheel over once or twice during the ripening time.

i) The wheel should be ready to serve after 5 to 6 weeks. You can check by cutting out a small $\frac{1}{4}$-inch wedge. The cheese should feel soft and begin to ooze out of the rind, and it should taste and smell mild.

j) Press a small piece of waxed paper into the cut section before rewrapping. The cheese will keep for 6 to 8 weeks in the refrigerator.

73. Bucheron

MAKES Two 8-ounce logs

Ingredients
- Penicillium candidum mold powder
- 1¾ teaspoons sea salt
- 1 gallon pasteurized goat's milk
- 1 teaspoon Aroma B powdered mesophilic starter culture
- Pinch of Geotrichum candidum 15 mold powder
- 1 teaspoon calcium chloride diluted in ¼ cup cool nonchlorinated water
- 1 teaspoon liquid rennet diluted in ¼ cup cool nonchlorinated water

Directions
a) Twelve hours before starting, combine a pinch of P. candidum, ¼ teaspoon of the salt, and 2 cups of cool nonchlorinated water in an atomizer or spray bottle. Store at 50°F to 55°F.

b) In a non-reactive 6-quart stockpot, heat the milk over low heat to 72°F; this should take about 10 minutes.

c) Sprinkle the starter, $\frac{1}{8}$ teaspoon of P. candidum mold powder, and the Geotrichum candidum mold powder over the milk and let rehydrate for 5 minutes. Mix well using a whisk in an up-and-down motion for 20 strokes. Add the calcium chloride and gently whisk in for 1 minute, then add the rennet in the same way. Cover and let sit, maintaining 72°F, for 18 hours, or until the curds are a firm mass and whey is coating on top.

d) Place a draining rack over a tray. Steady 2 cylindrical Saint-Maure or bûche molds inside 2 round, straight-sided molds and place on the rack.

e) Gently cut $\frac{1}{2}$-inch-thick slices of curds using a ladle or skimmer and gently ladle the slices into the cylindrical mold. Let drain until more curds can be added to the molds. Do not be tempted to add another mold; the curds will compress as the whey drains out, making room for all of the curds.

f) When all the curds have been ladled into the molds, cover them with a clean kitchen towel and let the cheeses drain for 24 hours at room temperature. Remove any collected whey a few times while draining, wiping out the tray with a paper towel each time.

g) After 6 hours, or when the cheeses are firm enough to handle, gently invert the molds onto your palm to tip the cheeses in their molds. Do this a few more times during the 24 hours to aid in uniform formation of the cheeses and development of the bacteria. At the end of 24 hours, the curds will have reduced to about half the height of the molds.

h) Once the cheeses have stopped draining and the curds have compressed to below the halfway point of the mold, place a mat in a ripening box. Remove the cheeses from the molds and sprinkle $\frac{3}{4}$ teaspoon of the salt over the entire surface of each cheese.

i) Set the cheeses at least 1 inch apart on the mat in the ripening box and allow 10 minutes for the salt to dissolve, then mist lightly with the P. candidum solution.

Wipe any moisture from the walls of the box. Cover the box loosely with the lid and let it stand at room temperature for 24 hours.

j) Drain any whey and wipe out any moisture from the box, then ripen the cheese at 50°F to 55°F and 90 percent humidity for 2 weeks. For the first few days, adjust the lid to be slightly open for a portion of each day to maintain the desired humidity level.

k) Too much humidity will create an undesirably wet surface. The surface of the cheese should appear moist but not wet. Each day, wipe out any moisture that may have accumulated in the ripening box. Throughout the ripening period, turn the cheeses one-quarter turn daily to maintain their log shape.

l) After 2 days, very lightly mist with the mold solution. After about 5 days, the first signs of white fuzzy mold will appear. After 10 to 14 days, the cheeses will be fully coated in white mold. Remove any undesirable mold using a piece of cheesecloth dipped in a vinegar-salt solution.

m) Clean and dry the ripening box, wrap the cheeses in cheese paper, and return them to the ripening box. The cheeses will begin to soften within 1 week or so.

n) After a total of 4 weeks from the start of ripening, wrap in plastic wrap and store in the refrigerator. It is best to consume this cheese when it has reached the desired ripeness, between 4 weeks and 5 weeks.

74. Camembert

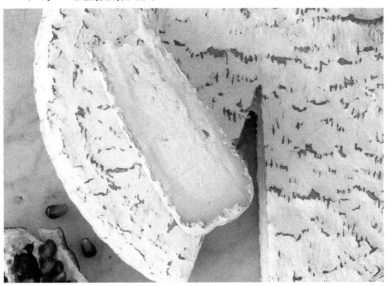

MAKES 1 pound

Ingredients

- 3 quarts pasteurized whole cow's milk
- 1 teaspoon MM 100 powdered mesophilic starter culture
- $\frac{1}{8}$ teaspoon Penicillium candidum mold powder
- 1 teaspoon calcium chloride diluted in $\frac{1}{4}$ cup cool nonchlorinated water
- 1 teaspoon liquid rennet diluted in $\frac{1}{4}$ cup cool nonchlorinated water
- 5 tablespoons kosher salt

Directions

a) In a nonreactive 6-quart stockpot, heat the milk over low heat to 90°F; this should take about 20 minutes. Turn off the heat.

b) Sprinkle the starter and mold powder over the milk and let rehydrate for 5 minutes. Mix well using a whisk in an up-and-down motion.

c) Cover and maintain 90°F, letting the milk ripen for $1\frac{1}{2}$ hours. Add the calcium

chloride and gently whisk in, then add
the rennet in the same way. Cover and
let sit, maintaining 90°F, until the curds
give a clean break.

d) Cut the curds into $\frac{1}{4}$- to $\frac{1}{2}$-inch pieces
and let sit for 5 minutes. Gently stir
with a rubber spatula to prevent the
curd from matting together, then ladle o
one-third of the whey. Add the salt and
gently stir to incorporate.

e) Ladle the curds into a 4-inch Camembert
mold set on a draining rack over a tray.
Let drain at room temperature until the
cheese is firm enough to tip, about 2
hours. Flip the cheese every hour for 5
hours, or until it stops draining.

75. Coulommiers

MAKES Four 5-ounce cheeses

Ingredients

- Penicillium candidum mold powder
- 3½ teaspoons kosher salt
- 2 gallons pasteurized whole cow's milk
- 1 teaspoon MA 4001 powdered mesophilic starter culture
- 1 teaspoon calcium chloride diluted in ¼ cup cool nonchlorinated water
- 1 teaspoon liquid rennet diluted in ¼ cup cool nonchlorinated water

Directions

a) Twelve hours before starting, combine a pinch of P. candidum, ½ teaspoon of salt, and 1 quart of nonchlorinated water in an atomizer or spray bottle. Store at 50°F to 55°F.

b) In a nonreactive 10-quart stockpot, heat the milk over low heat to 90°F; this should take about 20 minutes.

c) Sprinkle the starter and ⅛ teaspoon of P. candidum mold powder over the milk and let rehydrate for 5 minutes. Mix well using a whisk in an up-and-down motion. Add the calcium chloride and gently whisk in, then add the rennet in the same way. Cover and let sit, maintaining 90°F for $1\frac{1}{2}$ hours, or until the curds give a clean break.

d) Cut the curds into $\frac{1}{2}$-inch thick slices and let sit for 5 minutes to firm up the curds. Using a rubber spatula, gently stir around the edges of the pot for 5 minutes to shrink the curds slightly and keep them from matting.

e) Set a draining rack over a tray, put a cutting board on the rack and a cheese mat on the board, and, place four 4-inch Camembert molds on the mat. Using a skimmer, gently ladle the slices of curds into the molds. Fill the molds to the top, then continue to add slices as the curds drain.

f) When all the curds have been transferred to the molds, cover the molds with a clean kitchen towel and let drain at room temperature for 5 to 6 hours, or until the curds have reduced to almost half the height of the molds. Discard the whey periodically.

g) Place a second mat and cutting board over the top of the molds. With one hand holding the top board Warmly against the mat and molds, lift and gently tip over the bottom board and mat with the molds and place back onto the draining rack; the second board and mat will now be on the bottom and the original mat and board will be on top.

h) Let drain for 6 hours, until the curds are about $1\frac{1}{2}$ to 2 inches high, then tip again and let drain for another 3 hours. Stop tipping once the cheeses stop draining; they should be well drained and firm to the touch.

i) Remove the molds and sprinkle about $1\frac{1}{2}$ teaspoons salt over the tops and sides of the cheeses. Leave for 10 minutes, allowing the salt to dissolve. Place the cheeses salt side down on a clean cheese mat in a ripening box and salt the other sides, again using about $1\frac{1}{2}$ teaspoons.

Cover the box with the lid slightly open for a little air circulation and ripen the cheeses at 50°F to 55°F and 90 percent humidity. High humidity is essential for making this cheese.

j) Flip the cheeses daily, removing any whey and any moisture that may have accumulated in the ripening box, as moisture will inhibit the proper white mold development. Once moisture no longer accumulates in the box, cover the box tightly.

k) After 2 days, spray lightly with the mold solution. After about 5 days, the first signs of white fuzzy mold will appear. After 10 to 14 days, the cheeses will be fully coated in white mold. Remove any undesirable mold using a piece of cheesecloth dipped in a vinegar-salt solution.

l) Clean the ripening box, wrap the cheeses in cheese paper, and return them to the ripening box. The cheese will begin to soften within 1 week or so. It is ready to eat when the center feels soft to the touch; this can be 1 to 2 weeks or slightly longer. Store in the refrigerator until they reach the desired ripeness.

76.   Craggy cloaked cabra

MAKES Ten 3-ounce cheeses

Ingredients

- Penicillium candidum mold powder
- 4¼ teaspoons sea salt
- 1 gallon pasteurized goat's milk
- 1 teaspoon Aroma B powdered mesophilic starter culture Pinch of Geotrichum candidum 15 mold powder
- 1 teaspoon calcium chloride diluted in ¼ cup cool nonchlorinated water
- 1 teaspoon liquid rennet diluted in ¼ cup cool nonchlorinated water
- 2 tablespoons vegetable ash

Directions

a) Twelve hours before starting, combine a pinch of P. candidum, ¼ teaspoon of the salt, and 2 cups of cool nonchlorinated water in an atomizer or spray bottle. Store at 50°F to 55°F.

b) In a nonreactive 6-quart stockpot, heat the milk over low heat to 72°F; this should take about 10 minutes. Turn off the heat.

c) Sprinkle the starter, $\frac{1}{8}$ teaspoon of P. candidum, and the Geotrichum candidum mold powder over the milk and let rehydrate for 5 minutes. Mix well using a whisk in an up-and-down motion for 20 strokes. Cover and maintain 72°F, letting the milk ripen for 30 minutes. Add the calcium chloride and gently whisk in for 1 minute, then add the rennet in the same way. Cover and let sit, maintaining 72°F for 8 to 10 hours, or until the curds give a clean break.

d) Cut the curds into $\frac{1}{2}$-inch pieces and let sit for 5 minutes. Gently stir for 10 minutes with a rubber spatula, then ladle the curds into a colander lined with damp butter muslin and let drain for 30 minutes. Sprinkle in 1 tablespoon of the salt and gently toss with your hands to incorporate, then make a draining sack from the muslin and let drain for 4 hours, or until the whey stops dripping.

e) Using a scale, portion the drained curds into 10 pieces; each should weigh approximately $3\frac{1}{2}$ ounces. Lightly shape and roll into balls, then place the cheeses at least 1 inch apart on a mat set in a ripening box. Cover the box loosely with the lid and let stand at room temperature for 8 hours.

f) Drain the whey and wipe out any moisture from the box, then ripen the cheese at 50°F to 55°F and 85 percent humidity for 2 days. Adjust the lid to be slightly open for a portion of each day to maintain the desired humidity level. The surface of the cheese should appear moist but not wet.

g) In a small bowl or jar, combine the vegetable ash with the remaining 1 teaspoon of salt. Wearing disposable gloves, use a mesh strainer to dust the cheeses with the vegetable ash, coating them completely. Gently pat the ash onto the surface of the cheeses. Place the dusted cheeses on a clean cheese mat in a dry ripening box. Ripen at 50°F to 55°F and 85 percent humidity, turning the cheeses daily to maintain the round shape.

h) Two days after you have washed the cheeses, very lightly mist them with the mold solution. Secure the lid on the ripening box. After about 5 days, the first signs of white fuzzy mold will appear through the ash. After 10 to 14 days, the cheeses will be fully coated in white mold. The wrinkled surface will also begin to develop within 10 days.

i) At 2 weeks, clean and dry the ripening box, wrap the cheeses in cheese paper, and return them to the ripening box. The cheeses will begin to soften within 1 week or so. After a total of 3 weeks from the start of ripening, store them in the refrigerator. It is best to consume these cheeses when they have reached the desired ripeness, about 3 to 4 weeks from the start of ripening.

77. Crottin

MAKES Four 3½-ounce cheeses

Ingredients

- 1 gallon pasteurized goat's milk
- 1 teaspoon Meso I or Aroma B powdered mesophilic starter culture Pinch of Penicillium candidum mold powder
- Pinch of Geotrichum candidum 15 mold powder
- 1 teaspoon calcium chloride diluted in ¼ cup cool nonchlorinated water
- 1 teaspoon liquid rennet diluted in ¼ cup cool nonchlorinated water
- 1 tablespoon sea salt

Directions

a) Let the milk sit at room temperature for 1 hour. In a nonreactive 6-quart stockpot, heat the milk over low heat to 72°F; this should take about 10 minutes. Turn off the heat.

b) Sprinkle the starter and the mold powders over the milk and let rehydrate for 5 minutes. Mix well using a whisk in an up-and-down motion. Add the calcium chloride and gently whisk in for 1 minute, then add the rennet in the same way. Cover and maintain 72°F, letting the milk ripen for 18 hours, or until the curds form a solid mass.

c) Place 4 crottin molds on a draining rack set over a tray. Gently cut $\frac{1}{2}$-inch-thick slices of the curds using a ladle or skimmer and gently ladle the slices of curds into the molds. Drain until more curds can be added to the molds. Do not be tempted to add another mold; the curds will compress as the whey drains out, making room for all of the curds.

d) When all of the curds have been ladled into the molds, cover them with a clean kitchen towel and let the cheeses drain at room temperature. Remove any collected whey a few times while draining, wiping out the tray with a paper towel each time.

e) After 12 hours, or when the cheeses are Warm enough to handle, gently invert the molds onto your palm to tip the cheeses in their molds. Do this three more times during the next 36 hours to aid in uniform formation of the cheeses and development of the bacteria. After 48 hours, the curds will have reduced to about half the height of the mold.

f) Once the cheeses have stopped draining and the curds have compressed to below the halfway point of the mold, place a mat in a ripening box. Remove the cheeses from the molds and sprinkle the salt over the tops and bottoms of the cheeses. Set them at least 1 inch apart on the mat in the ripening box and allow 10 minutes for the salt to dissolve. Wipe any moisture from the walls of the box.

g) Cover the box loosely with the lid and let it stand at room temperature for 8 hours. Drain any whey and wipe out any moisture from the box, then ripen the cheeses at 50°F to 55°F and 90 percent humidity, Hipping the cheeses daily.

h) For the rest few days, adjust the lid to be slightly open for a portion of each day to maintain the desired humidity level. Too much humidity will create an undesirably wet surface. The surface of the cheeses should appear moist but not wet.

i) After about 5 days, the first signs of white fuzzy mold will appear. After 10 to 14 days, the cheeses will be fully coated in white mold. Clean and dry the ripening box, wrap the cheeses in cheese paper, and return them to the ripening box.

j) The cheeses will begin to soften within 1 week or so. After a total of 3 weeks from the start of ripening, wrap the cheeses in fresh cheese paper and store in the refrigerator. It is best to consume these cheeses when they have reached the desired ripeness, between 3 and 4 weeks from the beginning of ripening.

78. Fromage à l'Huile

MAKES Four 6-ounce crottin disks

Ingredients

- 2 gallons pasteurized goat's milk
- 1 teaspoon MM 100 or MA 011 powdered mesophilic starter culture Pinch of Choozit CUM yeast
- Pinch of Penicillium candidum mold powder Pinch of Geotrichum candidum 17 mold powder
- $\frac{1}{4}$ teaspoon calcium chloride diluted in $\frac{1}{2}$ cup cool nonchlorinated water $\frac{1}{4}$ teaspoon liquid rennet diluted in $\frac{1}{2}$ cup cool nonchlorinated water
- 2 teaspoons kosher salt

Directions

a) In a nonreactive 10-quart stockpot, heat the milk over medium heat to 75°F; this should take about 12 minutes. Turn off the heat.

b) Sprinkle the starter, yeast, and mold powders over the milk and let rehydrate for 5 minutes. Mix well using a whisk in an up-and-down motion.

c) Cover and maintain 75°F, letting the milk ripen for 25 minutes. Gently whisk in the calcium chloride for 1 minute, and then add the rennet in the same way.

d) Cover and let sit, maintaining 75°F for 15 to 20 hours, until the pH of the whey is below 4.6 but not lower than 4.4. At this point, the curds will have separated from the sides of the vat and there will be cracks in the body of the curds and a $\frac{1}{2}$-inch layer of whey on top of the curds.

e) Set a draining rack over a tray and place 4 crottin molds on the rack. The curd can be ladled in large scoops and drained in damp cheesecloth for 10 to 15 hours and then packed into the crottin molds or gently ladled in small scoops directly into the molds. Either way, once the curds are in the molds, let them drain for 15 to 36 hours at room temperature.

f) Sprinkle $\frac{1}{4}$ teaspoon of kosher salt over the top of each cheese in its mold. After about 10 hours of draining, the curds will be firm and hold their shape.

g) After 12 hours total draining time, unmold the cheeses, and return them to the molds and the rack to drain further. Sprinkle another $\frac{1}{4}$ teaspoon of salt over the top of each cheese in its mold.

h) Unmold the cheeses and set them on a cheese mat to air-dry at 60°F to 65°F. Flip the cheeses the next day, then let them sit until there is visible mold growth on the surface; this should take 3 to 5 days.

i) When there is growth, tip the cheeses over and move them to a more humid and colder place, in a ripening box at 45°F to 48°F and 90 percent humidity. Flip the cheeses daily until they are completely covered with white mold; this should happen within 10 days.

j) After a total of 2 weeks from the start of ripening, wrap the cheeses in cheese paper and store in the refrigerator.

k) It is best to consume these cheeses when they have reached the desired

ripeness, between 2 and 3 weeks from
the beginning of ripening, or longer for a
stronger flavor.

79. Mushroom-infused camembert

MAKES Two 8-ounce cheeses

Ingredients

- Penicillium candidum mold powder
- $4\frac{1}{2}$ teaspoons kosher salt
- 1 ounce dried sliced shiitake mushrooms 1 gallon pasteurized whole cow's milk
- $\frac{1}{4}$ teaspoon MM 100 powdered mesophilic starter culture Pinch of Geotrichum candidum 15 mold powder
- $\frac{1}{4}$ teaspoon calcium chloride diluted in $\frac{1}{4}$ cup cool nonchlorinated water
- $\frac{1}{4}$ teaspoon liquid rennet diluted in $\frac{1}{4}$ cup cool nonchlorinated water

Directions

a) Twelve hours before starting, combine a pinch of P. candidum, $\frac{1}{2}$ teaspoon of salt, and 1 quart of cool nonchlorinated water in an atomizer or spray bottle. Store at 50°F to 55°F.

b) In a nonreactive 6-quart stockpot, stir the mushrooms into the milk, then heat over low heat to 110°F to 112°F. Turn off the heat and maintain temperature for

55 minutes. Strain the milk through a fine-mesh strainer, pressing down on the mushrooms to squeeze out any liquid. Discard the mushrooms.

c) Cool the milk to 90°F, then sprinkle the starter, $\frac{1}{8}$ teaspoon of P. candidum mold powder, and the Geotrichum candidum mold powder over the milk and let rehydrate for 5 minutes. Mix well using a whisk in an up-and-down motion. Add the calcium chloride and gently whisk in, then add the rennet in the same way. Cover and let sit, maintaining a temperature of 85°F for $1\frac{1}{2}$ hours, or until the curds give a clean break.

d) 4. Cut the curds into $\frac{1}{2}$-inch pieces and let sit for 5 minutes to firm up. Using a rubber spatula, gently stir around the edges of the pot for 5 minutes to shrink the curds and keep them from matting. Let the curds rest for 5 minutes; they will sink to the bottom.

e) Set a draining rack over a tray, put a cutting board on the rack and a cheese mat on the board, and, finally, place the two 4-inch Camembert molds on the mat. Ladle o some of the whey and, using a skimmer, gently ladle the curds into the molds. Let drain for 2 hours, until the curds have reduced to about half the height of the molds.

f) Place a second mat and cutting board over the top of the molds. With one hand holding the top board firmly against the mat and molds, lift and gently tip the molds over and set them back onto the draining rack.

g) Let drain for 2 hours, then tip again. At this point the curds should be $1\frac{1}{2}$ to 2 inches high. Cover and let drain at room temperature for 8 hours or overnight. Flip the cheeses again and let drain for 2 more hours.

h) Remove the molds and sprinkle about 2 teaspoons of salt over the top and sides of the cheeses. Leave for 10 minutes, allowing the salt to dissolve. At this point, spray lightly with the mold solution. Place the cheeses salt side down on a clean mat in a ripening box and salt the other side, using the remaining 2 teaspoons of salt.

i) Cover the box with the lid slightly open for a little air circulation and ripen the cheeses at 50°F to 55°F and 90 percent humidity. High humidity is essential for making this cheese.

j) Flip the cheeses daily, removing any whey and any moisture that may have accumulated in the ripening box. Keep covered to maintain the humidity level.

k) After about 5 days, the first signs of white fuzzy mold will appear. Continue to tip the cheeses daily.

l) After 10 to 14 days, the cheeses will be fully coated in white mold. Wrap them loosely in cheese paper and return them to the ripening box at 50°F to 55°F and 85 percent humidity. The cheeses will begin to soften within 1 week or so.

m) After a total of 4 weeks from the start of ripening, move the cheeses to the refrigerator until they reach the desired ripeness, up to 6 weeks from the start of ripening.

80. Bloomy robiola

MAKES 2 pounds

Ingredients

- Robiola
- 1 gallon pasteurized whole cow's milk
- 1 gallon pasteurized goat's milk
- 1 teaspoon MM 100 powdered mesophilic starter culture
- 1 teaspoon Geotrichum candidum 15 mold powder
- 1 teaspoon calcium chloride diluted in $\frac{1}{4}$ cup cool nonchlorinated water 4 drops rennet diluted in $\frac{1}{4}$ cup nonchlorinated water
- Kosher salt

Directions

a) In a nonreactive 10-quart stockpot, heat the milks over low heat to 95°F; this should take about 25 minutes. Turn off the heat.

b) Sprinkle the starter and mold powder over the milks and let rehydrate for 5 minutes. Mix well using a whisk in an up-and-down motion. Add the calcium chloride and gently whisk in, and then add the rennet in the same way. Cover and let sit, maintaining 95°F for up to 18 hours, or until the curds give a clean break.

c) Set a draining rack over a tray, followed by a cheese mat. Place 2 Camembert molds on the mat. Using a skimmer, gently ladle the curds into the molds. Let drain at room temperature for 8 to 10 hours, or until the curds have compressed to $1\frac{1}{2}$ to 2 inches.

d) Sprinkle $\frac{1}{4}$ teaspoon of kosher salt over the top of each cheese in its mold. After 10 to 12 hours of draining, the curds will be firm and hold their shape. Unmold the cheeses, tip them, and return them to the rack to drain further. Sprinkle another $\frac{1}{4}$ teaspoon of salt over the top of each cheese.

e) Let the cheeses drain for 2 hours, then place the cheeses on a clean cheese mat in a ripening box. Cover the box with its lid and let ripen at 77°F and 92 to 95 percent humidity. Every 8 hours, loosen the lid to allow air to circulate.

f) After 30 to 48 hours, lower the temperature to 55°F and keep the humidity at 92 to 95 percent.

g) After about 5 days, the signs of a creamy white surface will appear. Continue to Pip the cheeses daily and remove any excess moisture from the box. After 7 to 10 days, the cheeses will have a rosy surface hue. After 3 to 4 weeks some blue mold may have formed on the surface.

h) At this point the cheese will be very ripe, and barely contained by its thin rind. You may use the cheeses now, wrap and store them in the refrigerator, or continue aging for up to 3 months.

81. Saint-marcellin

MAKES Four 3-ounce rounds

Ingredients

- 3 quarts pasteurized whole cow's milk
- 1 teaspoon Meso II powdered mesophilic starter culture Pinch of Penicillium candidum mold powder
- Pinch of Geotrichum candidum 15 mold powder
- $\frac{1}{4}$ teaspoon calcium chloride diluted in $\frac{1}{4}$ cup cool nonchlorinated water 6 drops liquid rennet diluted in $\frac{1}{4}$ cup cool nonchlorinated water
- 3 teaspoons kosher salt

Directions

a) In a nonreactive 4-quart stockpot, heat the milk over low heat to 75°F; this should take about 12 minutes. Turn off the heat.

b) Sprinkle the starter and mold powders over the milk and let rehydrate for 5 minutes. Mix well using a whisk in an up-and-down motion. Add the calcium chloride and gently whisk in, then add

365

the rennet in the same way. Cover and let sit, maintaining 72°F to 75°F for 12 hours.

c) Cut the curds into $\frac{1}{2}$-inch slices using a ladle or skimmer. Using a rubber spatula, gently stir around the edges of the pot, then let the curds stand for 5 minutes.

d) Set a draining rack over a tray, then place 4 Saint-Marcellin molds on the rack. Ladle the curds into a colander or strainer lined with damp butter muslin and let drain for 15 minutes. Ladle the curds into the molds up to their tops, then let drain until more curds can be added to the molds.

e) Do not be tempted to add another mold; the curds will compress as the whey drains out. The process will take about 30 minutes. Drain the curds at room temperature. After 6 hours, tip the cheeses in the molds and sprinkle the tops with $1\frac{1}{2}$ teaspoons of the salt. Let drain for another 6 hours, then tip the cheeses in the molds again and sprinkle the tops with the remaining $1\frac{1}{2}$ teaspoons of salt and drain for another 6 hours.

f) Unmold the cheeses and place them on a cheese mat in a ripening box. Cover the box loosely and let the cheeses drain at room temperature for 48 hours, tipping the cheeses daily and removing any whey that has accumulated.

g) Ripen at 55°F and 90 percent humidity for 14 days, or until a white fuzzy mold has developed to cover the cheese, Yipping the cheeses daily and continuing to remove the whey. The cheeses are ready to eat at this point, or they can be aged further.

h) Place each disk in a shallow clay crock and cover with plastic wrap or the crock's lid. If crocks are not used, wrap the cheeses in cheese paper or plastic wrap and store in the refrigerator for up to 6 weeks.

82. Valençay

MAKES Four 3- to 4-ounce pyramid-shaped cheeses

Ingredients
- 1 gallon pasteurized goat's milk
- 1 teaspoon Meso I or Aroma B powdered mesophilic starter culture $\frac{1}{8}$ teaspoon Penicillium candidum mold powder
- Pinch of Geotrichum candidum 15 mold powder
- 1 teaspoon calcium chloride diluted in $\frac{1}{4}$ cup cool nonchlorinated water
- 1 teaspoon liquid rennet diluted in $\frac{1}{4}$ cup cool nonchlorinated water
- 1 cup vegetable ash powder
- 2 teaspoons sea salt

Directions
a) In a nonreactive 6-quart stockpot, heat the milk over low heat to 72°F; this should take about 10 minutes. Turn off the heat.
b) Sprinkle the starter and mold powders over the surface of the milk and let

rehydrate for 5 minutes. Mix well using a whisk in an up-and-down motion. Add the calcium chloride and gently whisk in for 1 minute, then add the rennet in the same way. Cover and let sit, maintaining 72°F for 12 hours, or until the curds give a clean break.

c) Cut the curds into $\frac{1}{2}$-inch slices using a ladle or skimmer. Using a rubber spatula, gently stir around the edges of the pot for 5 minutes, then let the curds stand for 5 minutes.

d) Set a draining rack on a tray, then place 4 truncated pyramid molds on the rack. Ladle the slices of curds into the molds, then let drain until more curds can be added to the molds. Do not be tempted to add another mold; the curds will compress as the whey drains out.

e) Cover with a dish towel and let the cheeses drain for 48 hours at room temperature, removing any whey a few times while draining and removing any collected whey with a paper towel each time you drain it. Flip the molds after 12 hours or when the cheeses are firm enough to handle, then tip a few more times during the next 36 hours. At the end of 48 hours, the curds will have reduced to about half the height of the mold.

f) Remove the molds and combine the vegetable ash with the salt in a small bowl. Wearing disposable gloves, use a One-mesh strainer to dust the cheeses with vegetable ash, lightly coating each completely. Gently pat the ash onto the surface of the cheeses.

g) Place the cheeses at least 1 inch apart on a clean cheese mat in a ripening box. Cover loosely with the lid and let stand at room temperature for 24 hours. Wipe out any moisture from the box, then ripen at 50°F to 55°F and 90 percent humidity for 3 weeks.

h) For the first few days, adjust the lid to be slightly open for a portion of each day to maintain the desired humidity level. The surface of the cheeses should appear moist but not wet.

i) Continue to tip the cheeses daily. After about 5 days, the first signs of white fuzzy mold will appear through the ash. After 10 to 14 days the cheeses will be fully coated in white mold. As the cheese continues to age, the surface will turn a very light gray.

j) Wrap the cheeses in cheese paper and return them to the ripening box; they will begin to soften within 1 week or so. After a total of 4 weeks from the start of ripening, wrap the cheeses in fresh cheese paper and store them in the refrigerator. It is best to consume this cheese when it has reached the desired ripeness, within 4 to 6 weeks from the start of ripening.

WASHED-RIND AND SMEARED-RIND CHEESES

83. Ale-washed coriander trappist cheese

MAKES 1 pound

Ingredients

- 1 gallon pasteurized whole cow's milk
- 1½ teaspoons coriander seeds, crushed
- 1½ teaspoons granulated orange peel
- 1 teaspoon Meso II powdered mesophilic starter culture
- 1 teaspoon calcium chloride diluted in ¼ cup cool nonchlorinated water
- 1 teaspoon liquid rennet diluted in ¼ cup cool nonchlorinated water
- Kosher salt
- One 12-ounce bottle Belgian ale at room temperature, plus 16 to 24 ounces more for washing

Directions

a) In a nonreactive 2-quart saucepan, heat 1 quart of the milk over low heat to 90°F; this should take about 20 minutes. Stir in 1 teaspoon of the coriander and 1 teaspoon of the orange peel, then slowly raise the temperature to 110°F over the course of 10 minutes. Turn off the heat, cover, and let steep for 45 minutes, or until the temperature drops back down to 90°F.

b) Place the remaining 3 quarts of milk in a nonreactive 6-quart stockpot. Pour the steeped milk through a fine-mesh strainer into the larger pot of milk and whisk to combine. Discard the coriander and orange. Bring the milk to 90°F over low heat; this should take 5 minutes.

c) Sprinkle the starter over the milk and let it rehydrate for 5 minutes. Mix well using a whisk in an up-and-down motion. Cover and maintain 90°F, allowing the milk to ripen for few minutes. Add the calcium chloride and gently whisk in for 1 minute, then add the rennet in the same way. Cover and let sit, maintaining 90°F for 1 hour, or until the curds give a clean break.

d) Still maintaining 90°F, cut the curds into $\frac{1}{2}$-inch pieces and let sit for 10 minutes. Gently stir the curds for 15 minutes to expel more whey, then let settle for another 10 minutes. The curds will shrink to the size of small beans. Meanwhile, heat 2 quarts of water to 175°F. Ladle enough whey to expose the curds. Add enough hot water to bring the temperature to 93°F.

e) Stir for 10 minutes. Repeat the process of removing whey and adding hot water, this time bringing the temperature to 100°F. Stir for 15 minutes, then let the curds settle for 10 minutes. Cover and let rest for 45 minutes, maintaining 100°F. The curds will mat and form a slab.

f) Drain enough whey to expose the slab of curds. Transfer the slab to a Vat-bottomed colander, place it over the pot, and let drain for 5 minutes. Transfer the slab to a cutting board and cut into $\frac{3}{8}$-inch-thick slices. Place in a bowl and gently toss with 2 teaspoons of the salt.

g) Line a 5-inch tomme mold with damp cheesecloth and set it on a draining rack. Tightly pack half of the curds in the mold, cover with the cloth tails and the follower, and press at 5 pounds for 10 minutes, just to compact the curds slightly. Peel back the cloth and sprinkle on the remaining ½ teaspoon of coriander and ½ teaspoon of orange peel, then pack in the rest of the milled curds.

h) Cover with the cloth tails and the follower and press at 8 pounds for 6 hours at room temperature. Remove the cheese from the mold, unwrap, tip, and redress, then press again at 8 pounds for 8 hours to thoroughly compress the curds.

i) Pour the bottle of ale into a lidded nonreactive container large enough to hold both ale and cheese. Remove the cheese from the mold and cheesecloth and place in the ale. Soak the cheese, covered, for 8 hours at 55°F, tipping once.

j) Remove the cheese from the ale and pat dry. Reserve and refrigerate the ale and place the cheese on a cheese mat. Air-dry at room temperature for 12 hours. Return the cheese to the ale and soak for another 12 hours at 55°F. Remove, pat dry, and air-dry at room temperature for 12 hours, or until the surface is dry to the touch. Discard the ale.

k) Prepare a brine-ale wash: boil $\frac{1}{2}$ cup of water and let it cool, and combine with $\frac{1}{2}$ cup of ale, then dissolve 1 teaspoon of salt in the liquid. Store in the refrigerator.

l) Place the cheese on a mat in a ripening box and ripen at 50°F and 90 percent humidity for 4 to 6 weeks. Flip the cheese daily for the first 2 weeks, then twice weekly thereafter.

m) After each tip, pour a little brine-ale wash into a small dish, dip a small piece of cheesecloth in it, and use it to wipe the surface of the cheese. Discard any unused brine-ale wash after 1 week and make a fresh batch. Also wipe away any moisture from the bottom, sides, and lid of the ripening box each time you tip the cheese.

n)   Wrap the cheese in cheese paper and store refrigerated for up to 1 month. If you vacuum-seal the cheese, remove it from the package and pat it dry before consuming it.

84. Cabra al vino

MAKES 1½ pounds

Ingredients

- 2 gallons pasteurized goat's milk
- ¼ teaspoon Meso II powdered mesophilic starter culture
- 1 teaspoon calcium chloride diluted in ¼ cup cool nonchlorinated water
- ¾ teaspoon liquid rennet diluted in ¼ cup cool nonchlorinated water
- Kosher salt
- One 750 ml bottle red wine, chilled to 55°F

Directions

a) In a nonreactive 10-quart stockpot, heat the milk over low heat to 90°F; this should take about 20 minutes.

b) Sprinkle the starter over the milk and let it rehydrate for 5 minutes. Mix well using a whisk in an up-and-down motion. Cover and maintain 90°F, letting the milk ripen for 30 minutes. Add the calcium chloride and gently whisk in for 1 minute, then add the rennet in the same way.

Cover and let sit, maintaining 90°F for 1 hour, or until the curds give a clean break.

c) Still maintaining 90°F, cut the curds into $\frac{3}{4}$-inch pieces and let sit for 5 minutes. Gently stir the curds for 20 minutes, then let settle.

d) Meanwhile, heat 2 quarts of water to 175°F. Ladle enough whey to expose the curds. Add enough hot water to bring the temperature to 93°F. Stir for 5 minutes. Repeat the process of removing whey and adding hot water, this time bringing the temperature to 102°F. Stir for 15 minutes, then let the curds settle for 10 minutes.

e) Cover and let rest for minutes, maintaining 102°F. The curds will mat slightly and form a slab.

f) Drain enough whey to expose the slab of curds. Using a mesh strainer or ladle, gently turn the curds over every 5 minutes for 15 minutes. Place the slab in a bowl and, using your hands, break it into $\frac{1}{2}$-inch pieces and gently toss with 2 teaspoon of the salt.

g) Line an 8-inch tomme mold with damp butter muslin and set it on a draining rack. Fill the mold with the milled curds, cover with the tails of the cloth and the follower, and press at 5 pounds for 8 hours at room temperature. Remove the cheese from the mold, unwrap, tip, and redress, then press again at 5 pounds for 8 hours at room temperature.

h) Pour the wine into a lidded nonreactive container large enough to hold both wine and cheese. Remove the cheese from the mold and cloth and place it in the wine. Soak the cheese, covered, for 12 hours at 55°F, tipping once.

i) Remove the cheese from the wine and pat dry. Reserve and refrigerate the wine and place the cheese on a cheese mat. Air-dry at room temperature for 12 hours. Return the cheese to the wine and soak for another 12 hours at 55°F. Remove, pat dry, and air-dry at room temperature for 12 hours, or until the surface is dry to the touch. Discard the wine.

j) Place the cheese on a mat in a ripening box and ripen at 50°F and 85 percent humidity for 6 weeks. Flip the cheese daily for the first 2 weeks, then twice weekly thereafter. After each tip, wipe the surface with a small piece of cheesecloth dipped in a small amount of brine wash: boil $\frac{1}{2}$ cup of water and let it cool, then add 1 teaspoon of salt and stir to dissolve.

k) Store in the refrigerator. The brine wash will control unwanted mold growth. Discard any unused brine wash after 1 week and make a fresh batch. Also wipe away any moisture from the bottom, sides, and lid of the ripening box each time you tip the cheese.

l) After 2 weeks of ripening, you may wax coat the cheese and refrigerate for the duration of the aging time: up to 6 weeks. After $3\frac{1}{2}$ weeks or so, the cheese will have a musty, winery-meets-cheese-shop aroma.

85. Desert sunset pavé

MAKES Two 10-ounce cheeses or one $1\frac{1}{2}$-pound cheese

Ingredients

- 2 gallons pasteurized whole cow's milk
- 1 teaspoon MA 4001 powdered mesophilic starter culture
- $\frac{1}{8}$ teaspoon Penicillium candidum mold powder
- Pinch of Geotrichum candidum 15 mold powder
- 1 teaspoon calcium chloride diluted in $\frac{1}{4}$ cup cool nonchlorinated water
- 1 teaspoon liquid rennet diluted in $\frac{1}{4}$ cup cool nonchlorinated water
- Kosher salt and washing
- Liquid annatto for brining and washing

Directions

a) In a nonreactive 10-quart stockpot, heat the milk over low heat to 90°F; this should take 20 minutes. Turn off the heat.

b) Sprinkle the starter and mold powders over the milk and let rehydrate for 5 minutes. Mix well using a whisk in an up-and-down motion. Cover and maintain 90°F, allowing the milk to ripen for 1 hour. Add the calcium chloride and gently whisk in, then add the rennet in the same way. Cover and let sit, maintaining 90°F for 30 minutes, or until the curds give a clean break.

c) Still maintaining 90°F, cut the curds into $\frac{3}{4}$-inch pieces and let sit for 5 minutes to firm up. Gently stir the curds for 30 minutes, removing 2 cups of whey every 10 minutes. Then let the curds settle for 10 minutes.

d) Line one 7-inch square Taleggio mold or two 4-inch square cheese molds with damp butter muslin. Place the molds on a draining rack over a tray and gently ladle the curds into the molds, pressing them into the corners with your hand. Cover the curds with the tails of cloth and cover the entire setup with a kitchen towel. Let drain for 6 hours in a warm spot in the kitchen. Remove the cheese from the mold, unwrap, tip, and redress, then let drain for 6 more hours.

e) Two hours before the end of the draining time, make a soaking brine by combining $2\frac{1}{2}$ cups of cool nonchlorinated water, $\frac{1}{2}$ cup of salt, and 8 drops of annatto in a lidded nonreactive container large enough to hold the brine and cheese.

f) Stir to dissolve the salt completely, then cool to 50°F to 55°F. Remove the cheese from the mold and cloth and place it in the brine. Soak the cheese, covered, at 50°F to 55°F for 8 hours, tipping at least once.

g) Remove the cheese from the brine and pat dry. Air-dry at room temperature on a cheese mat or rack for 24 hours, or until the surface is dry to the touch.

h) Place the cheese on a mat in a ripening box and ripen at 50°F and 85 percent humidity, tipping every other day. At least 2 hours before you Dip the cheese the rest time, make a brine wash by combining $1\frac{1}{2}$ teaspoons of salt, 3 drops of annatto, and 1 cup of cool nonchlorinated water in a sterilized glass jar; shake well to dissolve the salt, then chill to 50°F to 55°F.

i) After each tip, pour a little brine wash into a small dish, dip a small piece of cheesecloth in it, wring it out, and use it to wipe the surface of the cheese.

j) Discard any unused brine wash after 1 week and make a fresh batch. Also wipe away any moisture from the bottom, sides, and lid of the ripening box each time you tip the cheese. 8.

k) The rind will become crusty and firm, and in 10 to 14 days an orange color will develop; this will deepen as the cheeses age. After 4 weeks, the rind should be slightly moist and the center of the cheese should feel soft; at this point, it's ready to eat. Consume within 2 weeks.

86. Washed-rind teleme-style

MAKES 2 pounds

Ingredients

- 2 gallons pasteurized whole cow's milk
- 1 teaspoon MA 4001 powdered mesophilic starter culture
- 1 teaspoon calcium chloride diluted in $\frac{1}{4}$ cup cool nonchlorinated water
- 1 teaspoon liquid rennet diluted in $\frac{1}{4}$ cup cool nonchlorinated water
- 2 tablespoons kosher salt

Directions

a) In a nonreactive 10-quart stockpot, heat the milk over low heat to 86°F; this should take 15 minutes. Turn off the heat.

b) Sprinkle the starter over the milk and let it rehydrate for 5 minutes. Mix well using a whisk in an up-and-down motion. Cover and maintain 86°F, allowing the milk to ripen for 1 hour. Add the calcium chloride and gently whisk in for 1 minute, then add the rennet in the same way.

Cover and let sit, maintaining 86°F for 30 to 45 minutes, or until the curds give a clean break.

c) Cut the curds into 1½-inch pieces and let sit for 5 minutes. Over low heat, slowly bring the curds to 102°F over a 40-minute period, stirring continuously to prevent them from matting. The curds will release more whey, firm up, and shrink to the size of large lima beans.

d) Once 102°F is reached, remove from the heat, maintain the temperature, and let the curds rest undisturbed for 30 minutes. Heat 2 quarts of water to 120°F. Ladle o+ enough whey to expose the curds. Add enough hot water to bring the temperature to 104°F. Stir continuously for 15 minutes, or until the curds cling together when pressed in your hand.

e) Line a colander with damp butter muslin and place it over a bowl or bucket large enough to capture the whey, which can be discarded. Gently ladle the curds into the colander and rinse with cold nonchlorinated water to cool them. Let drain for 5 minutes, then sprinkle in 1 tablespoon of the salt and gently and thoroughly toss with your hands.

f) Place a mat on a draining rack set over a tray, then set a 7-inch square Taleggio mold on the mat. Put the sack of rinsed curds in the mold and press the curds into the corners. Cover the top of the curds with the cloth tails and press with your hands to mat the curds. Let drain at room temperature for 6 hours for moist cheese, or 8 hours for a firmer cheese. Flip the cheese once halfway through this draining period.

g) Remove the cheese from the mold and pat dry. Rub the surface of the cheese with the remaining 1 tablespoon of salt and place it back in the mold without the cloth. Return the mold to the mat on the draining rack for 12 hours, Dipping once in that time.

h) Remove the cheese from the mold and place in a ripening box at 50°F to 55°F and 85 percent humidity for at least 2 weeks, tipping the cheese daily for even ripening.

i) After 1 week, wash with a simple brine solution twice a week for up to 2 months of ripening time. When the desired ripeness is reached, wrap and refrigerate until ready to eat.

87. Lemon vodka spirited goat

MAKES 1½ pounds

Ingredients

- 2 gallons pasteurized goat's milk
- 1 teaspoon MM 100 powdered mesophilic starter culture
- ¼ teaspoon Thermo B powdered thermophilic starter culture Geotrichum candidum 15 mold powder
- ¼ teaspoon calcium chloride diluted in ¼ cup cool nonchlorinated water
- 1 teaspoon liquid rennet diluted in ¼ cup cool nonchlorinated water
- Kosher salt
- Pinch of Brevibacterium linens powder
- 1 cup Charbay Meyer Lemon Vodka or other lemon-infused vodka

Directions

a) In a nonreactive 10-quart stockpot, heat the milk over low heat to 90°F; this should take about 20 minutes. Turn off the heat.

b) Sprinkle both starters and a pinch of the mold powder over the milk and let rehydrate for 5 minutes. Mix well using a whisk in an up-and-down motion.

c) Cover and maintain 90°F, allowing the milk to ripen for 45 minutes. Add the calcium chloride and gently whisk in for 1 minute, then add the rennet in the same way. Cover and let sit, maintaining 90°F for 30 to 45 minutes, or until the curds give a clean break.

d) Still maintaining 90°F, cut the curds into $\frac{1}{2}$-inch pieces and let rest for 10 minutes. Gently stir the curds for 10 minutes, then let rest for 30 minutes. Slowly raise the temperature to 100°F over 30 minutes, stirring the curds every 5 minutes. Let the curds sit for about 10 minutes; they will sink to the bottom.

e) Ladle out enough whey to expose the curds, then gently ladle the curds into a colander lined with damp butter muslin and let drain for 5 minutes.

f) Line an 8-inch tomme mold or 7-inch square Taleggio mold with damp butter muslin and set on a draining rack. Transfer the curds to the mold, gently distributing and pressing into the mold with your hand. Cover the curds with the cloth tails and a follower and press at 3 pounds for 1 hour.

g) Remove the cheese from the mold, unwrap, tip, and redress, then press at 5 pounds for 12 hours, tipping once at 6 hours.

h) Make 2 quarts of saturated brine and chill to 50°F to 55°F. Remove the cheese from the mold and cloth and place it in the brine to soak at 50°F to 55°F for 8 hours, tipping at least once during the brining process.

i) Remove the cheese from the brine and pat it dry. Air-dry on a cheese mat at room temperature for 12 hours, or until the surface is dry.

j) Place the cheese on a mat in a ripening box and age at 50°F to 55°F and 90 percent humidity, tipping daily for 1 week. Each time you tip the cheese, wipe any moisture from the bottom, sides, and lid of the box.

k) After 1 week, begin washing the surface with bacterial wash. Twelve hours before the first washing, prepare the solution by dissolving $1\frac{1}{2}$ teaspoons of salt in 1 cup of cool nonchlorinated water in a sterilized glass jar. Add 1 pinch each of Geotrichum candidum mold powder and B. linens powder, whisk to incorporate, cover, and store at 55°F.

l) When ready to wash, pour $1\frac{1}{2}$ tablespoons of the bacterial wash into a small bowl, preserving the rest for another washing. Dip a small piece of cheesecloth into the solution, squeeze out the excess, and rub it all over the entire surface of the cheese. Using a paper towel, wipe any excess moisture from the ripening box. Tip the cheese over and return it to the ripening box. Discard any bacterial wash left in the bowl.

m) Wash the cheese twice a week for 2 months, alternating the bacterial wash with spirits. To wash with the vodka, pour a little vodka into a bowl, dip a small piece of cheesecloth in it, wring out, and rub it over the entire surface of the cheese.

n) Discard any vodka left in the bowl. The rind will become slightly sticky, and at 10 to 14 days a light orange color will develop, which will deepen as the cheese ages. At 2 months, the rind should be only slightly moist and the cheese should be soft to the touch in the center; it is now ready to eat. The cheese should be eaten within 3 months.

88. Époisses

MAKES Two ½-pound cheeses

Ingredients

- 1 gallon pasteurized whole cow's milk
- 1 teaspoon Meso II powdered mesophilic starter culture
- Pinch of Brevibacterium linens powder
- ¼ teaspoon calcium chloride diluted in ¼ cup cool nonchlorinated water
- 2 drops liquid rennet diluted in ¼ cup cool nonchlorinated water
- Kosher salt
- 3 cups Marc de Bourgogne brandy, other similar pomace brandy, or grappa

Directions

a) In a nonreactive 10-quart stockpot, heat the milk over low heat to 86°F; this should take about 15 minutes.

b) Sprinkle the starter and B. linens powder over the milk and let rehydrate for 5 minutes. Mix well using a whisk in an up-and-down motion. Cover and maintain 86°F, allowing the milk to ripen for 30 minutes. Add the calcium chloride and gently whisk in for 1 minute, then add the rennet in the same way. Cover and let the milk ripen for 4 hours at room temperature, until the curds give a clean break.

c) Over low heat, bring the curds back to 86°F. Cut the curds into $\frac{3}{4}$-inch pieces and let sit for 5 minutes. At this point the curds will be extremely soft.

d) Line two 4-inch Camembert molds with damp cheesecloth and set on a draining rack over a tray. Gently ladle the curds into the molds, cover with the cloth tails, and cover the entire setup with a kitchen towel. Let drain for 24 hours at room temperature, preferably in a warm spot in the kitchen. Once the drained curds have shrunk to half the height of the molds, Rip the cheeses over every 2 hours.

e) Remove the cheeses from the molds and cloth. Rub about 1 teaspoon of salt over the entire surface of each cheese. Air-dry at room temperature on a rack for

18 hours, until the surface is dry to the touch.

f) Place the cheeses on a mat in a ripening box and age at 50°F and 90 percent humidity, tipping every 3 days for 6 weeks. Before you Rip the cheese the first time, make a brine wash by dissolving 1 teaspoon of salt in $\frac{1}{2}$ cup of boiled water and cooling it to 50°F to 55°F.

g) Each time you tip the cheese, first use a paper towel to wipe any moisture from the surface of the cheese, then wipe the entire surface of the cheese with a small piece of cheesecloth dipped in the brine wash. Discard any unused brine wash. Also use a paper towel to wipe any moisture from the bottom, sides, and lid of the ripening box each time you tip the cheese.

h) After the first week, begin alternating the brine wash with a wash of diluted brandy.

i) Pour a little of the diluted brandy into a small dish, dip a small piece of cheesecloth in it, and rub it over the entire surface of the cheese. Discard any brandy wash left in the dish. At 3 weeks, begin alternating the brine wash with undiluted brandy.

j) Continue washing and Zipping the cheese every 3 days for 6 weeks' total. The rind will become slightly sticky and very aromatic, and at 10 to 14 days a pale orange color will develop; this will change to the color of the brandy used and deepen as the cheese ages. At 6 weeks, the rind should be moist but not sticky, the center of the cheese should feel very soft, and the paste should be runny. When the cheese is nearing the desired ripeness, transfer it to the traditional wooden cheese box to finish.

k) Move the cheese to the refrigerator when fully ripened, and consume within 2 weeks.

89. Morbier

MAKES 1¾ pounds

Ingredients

- 2 gallons pasteurized whole cow's milk
- 1 teaspoon Meso II powdered mesophilic starter culture
- Brevibacterium linens powder
- ½ teaspoon calcium chloride diluted in ¼ cup cool nonchlorinated water
- ½ teaspoon liquid rennet diluted in ¼ cup cool nonchlorinated water
- ⅛ teaspoon vegetable ash mixed with ⅛ teaspoon sea salt
- Kosher salt

Directions

a) In a nonreactive 10-quart stockpot, heat the milk over low heat to 90°F; this should take about 20 minutes. Turn off the heat.

b) Sprinkle the starter and a pinch of B. linens powder over the milk and let rehydrate for 5 minutes. Mix well using a whisk in an up-and-down motion. Cover and maintain 90°F, allowing the milk to ripen for 1 hour. Add the calcium chloride and gently whisk in for 1 minute, then add the rennet in the same way.

c) Cover and let sit, maintaining 90°F for 30 minutes, or until the curds give a clean break.

d) Maintaining 90°F, cut the curds into $\frac{3}{4}$-inch pieces and let sit for 5 minutes. Over very low heat, slowly raise the temperature to 100°F over 30 minutes, stirring a few times. Let the curds settle for about 10 minutes. Using a measuring cup, remove about half of the whey and replace with enough 110°F water so the curds reach 104°F. Gently stir for 5 minutes, then let the curds settle.

e) Line 2 colanders with damp butter muslin, divide the curds between them, and let drain for 20 minutes. Line a draining rack with damp paper towels, extending the towels a few inches beyond the edges of the rack, and place an 8-inch tomme mold on top. Line the mold with damp butter muslin.

f) Transfer the contents of 1 colander of drained curds to the mold and press the curds into the edges with your hands. Wearing disposable gloves, use a fine-mesh strainer to carefully dust the surface of the curds with ash to within $\frac{1}{2}$ inch of the edge.

g) The dampened paper towels should catch any stray ash. Gently add the second batch of curds on top of the ash layer and press into the edges with your hands. Pull up the cloth and smooth out any wrinkles, then cover the curds with the cloth tails and the follower and press at 5 pounds for 1 hour. Remove the cheese from the mold, unwrap, tip, and redress, then press at 8 pounds for 12 hours or overnight.

h) Make 2 quarts of near-saturated brine and chill to 50°F to 55°F. Remove the cheese from the mold and cloth and place in the brine to soak at 50°F to 55°F for 6 hours, Kipping at least once during the brining process.

i) Remove the cheese from the brine and pat dry. Place it on a cheese mat and air-dry at room temperature for 12 hours, or until the surface is dry to the touch.

j) Place the cheese on a mat in a ripening box to age at 50°F to 55°F and 85 to 90 percent humidity for 1 week. Flip daily, using a paper towel to wipe away any accumulated moisture in the box each time you tip the cheese.

k) After 1 week, wash the surface with bacterial wash. Twelve hours before this washing, prepare the solution: Boil $\frac{1}{2}$ cup of water and let it cool in a glass jar, then add 1 teaspoon of kosher salt and stir to dissolve.

l) Add a small pinch of B. linens powder, cover the jar with the lid, and gently agitate to dissolve. Set aside at room temperature for the bacteria to rehydrate.

m) When ready to wash, pour $1\frac{1}{2}$ tablespoons of the bacterial wash into a small bowl, preserving the rest for another washing. Dip a small piece of cheesecloth into the solution, squeeze out the excess, and rub it over the entire surface of the cheese. tip the cheese over and return it to the ripening box. Discard any bacterial wash left in the bowl.

n) Two times a week, wash the cheese with a piece of cheesecloth dipped in simple brine or rub the surface of the cheese with a soft brush dipped in brine. Repeat this process twice a week for 2 months, tipping the cheese each time. The rind will become slightly sticky, and at 10 to 14 days a light orange color will develop, deepening to a tan shade as the cheese ages.

o) After 3 weeks, the paste under the surface at the edges of the cheese will begin to feel soft. Continue to wash or brush for 2 months.

p) At 2 months, the rind should be only slightly moist (not sticky) and the cheese should be soft to the touch; it is now ready to eat. Or, wrap the cheese in cheese paper and refrigerate to age for up to 2 more months if desired.

90.   Port salut

MAKES 1¼ pounds

Ingredients

- 6 quarts pasteurized whole cow's milk
- 1 teaspoon Meso II powdered mesophilic starter culture Brevibacterium linens powder
- 1 teaspoon calcium chloride diluted in ¼ cup cool nonchlorinated water
- 1 teaspoon liquid rennet diluted in ¼ cup cool nonchlorinated water Kosher salt

Directions

a) In a nonreactive 8-quart stockpot, heat the milk over low heat to 90°F; this should take about 20 minutes. Turn off the heat.

b) Sprinkle the starter and a pinch of B. linens powder over the milk and let rehydrate for 5 minutes. Mix well using a whisk in an up-and-down motion. Cover and maintain 90°F, allowing the milk to ripen for 1 hour. Add the calcium chloride and gently whisk in for 1 minute, then add the rennet in the same way.

Cover and let sit, maintaining 90°F for 30 minutes, or until the curds give a clean break.

c) Cut the curds into ½-inch pieces and let sit for 10 minutes. Meanwhile, heat 1 quart of water to 140°F. Ladle about one-third of the whey and replace with enough 140°F water to bring the temperature to 92°F. Gently stir for 10 minutes, then let the curds settle for 10 minutes. Repeat the process, again removing one-third of the whey and this time adding enough 140°F water to bring the temperature to 98°F. Gently stir for 10 minutes, then let the curds settle for 15 minutes.

d) Line a colander with damp cheesecloth, ladle the curds into it, and let drain for 10 minutes. Line a 5-inch tomme mold with damp cheesecloth and set it on a draining rack. Transfer the drained curds to the lined cheese mold, pressing the curds into the edges with your hand.

e) Pull up the cloth and smooth out any wrinkles, cover the curds with the cloth tails and follower, and press at 5 pounds for 30 minutes. Remove the cheese from the mold, unwrap, Tip, and redress, then press at 8 pounds for 12 hours or overnight.

f) Make 2 quarts of saturated brine and chill to 50°F to 55°F. Remove the cheese from the mold and cloth and place in the brine to soak at 50°F to 55°F for 8 hours, tipping at least once during the brining process.

g) Remove the cheese from the brine and pat dry. Place on a cheese mat and air-dry at room temperature for 12 hours. Place the cheese on a mat in a ripening box and age at 50°F to 55°F and 90 to 95 percent humidity, tipping daily for 1 week. Each time you tip the cheese, wipe any moisture from the bottom, sides, and lid of the ripening box with a paper towel.

h) After 1 week, begin washing the surface with bacterial wash. Twelve hours before the first washing, prepare the solution: Boil $\frac{1}{2}$ cup of water and let it cool in a glass jar, then add 1 teaspoon of kosher salt and stir to dissolve.

i) Add a small pinch of B. linens powder, cover the jar with the lid, and gently agitate to dissolve. Set aside at room temperature for the bacteria to rehydrate.

j) When ready to wash, pour $1\frac{1}{2}$ tablespoons of the bacterial wash into a small bowl, preserving the rest for another washing. Dip a small piece of cheesecloth into the solution, squeeze out the excess, and rub the entire surface of the cheese. tip the cheese over and return it to the ripening box. Discard any bacterial wash left in the bowl.

k) Repeat this process every 2 days, tipping the cheese each time. After you have washed the cheese with bacterial wash 4 times, switch to brine.

l) The rind will become slightly sticky, and at 10 to 14 days a light yellow-orange color will develop; this color will deepen as the cheese ages.

m) Continue to wash and ripen for 4 weeks' total. At this point the rind should be moist but not sticky and the center of the cheese should feel somewhat soft. Consume within 2 weeks of desired ripeness.

91. Reblochon

MAKES Two 1-pound cheeses

Ingredients

- 2 gallons pasteurized whole cow's milk
- 1 teaspoon Meso II powdered mesophilic starter culture
- $\frac{1}{8}$ teaspoon Brevibacterium linens powder
- 1 teaspoon calcium chloride diluted in $\frac{1}{4}$ cup cool nonchlorinated water
- 1 teaspoon liquid rennet diluted in $\frac{1}{4}$ cup cool nonchlorinated water
- Kosher salt

Directions

a) In a nonreactive 10-quart stockpot, heat the milk over low heat to 85°F; this should take about 15 minutes. Turn off the heat.

b) Sprinkle the starter and B. linens powder over the milk and let rehydrate for 5 minutes. Mix well using a whisk in an up-and-down motion. Cover and maintain 85°F, allowing the milk to ripen for 30 minutes. Add the calcium chloride and gently whisk in for 1 minute, then add the rennet in the same way. Cover and let sit, maintaining 85°F for 30 minutes, or until the curds give a clean break.

c) Still maintaining 85°F, cut the curds into $\frac{1}{2}$-inch pieces and let sit for 5 minutes. Slowly warm the curds to 95°F over 30 minutes, stirring every 10 minutes, then remove from the heat and let the curds settle.

d) Ladle out enough whey to expose the curds. Line two 5-inch tomme molds with damp cheesecloth and set them on a draining rack over a tray. Transfer the curds to the molds; you may have to mound them up in the molds, but they will all t in after 10 to 15 minutes of draining.

e) Let drain for 15 minutes, then pull up the cloth and smooth out any wrinkles. Cover the curds with the tails of cloth and the followers. Let drain on the rack for 30 minutes, then tip the cheeses, return them to the molds, and replace the followers. Flip every 20 minutes for 2 hours, then press at 5 pounds for 12 hours or overnight.

f) Remove the cheeses from the molds and cloth. Sprinkle 1 teaspoon of salt on the top and bottom of each cheese. Place the cheeses on a mat in a ripening box and age at 55°F and 90 percent humidity, tipping every other day.

g) Before you turn the cheese the first time, make a brine wash: boil $\frac{1}{2}$ cup of water and let it cool, then add 1 teaspoon of kosher salt and stir to dissolve. Store in the refrigerator. Each time you tip the cheese, wipe the surface with a small piece of cheesecloth dipped in a small amount of brine wash.

h) The brine wash will control unwanted mold growth. Discard any unused brine wash and make a fresh batch each week. Also wipe away any moisture from the bottom, sides, and lid of the ripening box each time you tip the cheese.

i) Continue tipping and washing the cheese every 2 days for 2 to 6 weeks. At 10 to

14 days, a light yellow-orange color will develop, deepening as the cheese ages. At 4 weeks, the rind should be moist but not sticky and the center of the cheese should feel soft.

j) Wrap the cheese in cheese paper, refrigerate when at the desired ripeness, and consume within 2 weeks of desired ripeness.

92. Taleggio

MAKES One 2-pound cheese or two 1-pound cheeses

Ingredients

- 2 gallons pasteurized whole cow's milk
- 1 teaspoon Meso II powdered mesophilic starter culture
- Pinch of Brevibacterium linens powder
- 1 teaspoon calcium chloride diluted in $\frac{1}{4}$ cup cool nonchlorinated water
- 1 teaspoon liquid rennet diluted in $\frac{1}{4}$ cup cool nonchlorinated water
- Kosher salt

Directions

a) Heat the milk in a nonreactive 10-quart stockpot over low heat to 90°F; this should take 20 minutes. Turn off the heat.

b) Sprinkle the starter and B. linens powder over the milk and let rehydrate for 5 minutes. Mix well using a whisk in an up-and-down motion. Cover and maintain 90°F, allowing the milk to ripen for 1 hour. Add the calcium chloride and gently whisk in for 1 minute, then add the rennet in the same way.

c) Cover and let sit, maintaining 90°F for 30 minutes, or until the curds give a clean break.

d) Still maintaining 90°F, cut the curds into $\frac{3}{4}$-inch pieces and let sit for 5 minutes. Gently stir the curds for 30 minutes, removing 2 cups of whey every 10 minutes. Then, let the curds rest undisturbed for 10 minutes.

e) Line one 7-inch square Taleggio mold or two 4-inch square bottomless cheese molds with damp cheesecloth and set on a draining rack over a tray. Gently ladle the curds into the molds, pressing them into the edges with your hand.

f) Cover with the tails of cloth and cover the entire setup with a kitchen towel. Let drain for 12 hours at room temperature, preferably in a warm spot in the kitchen. Every 2 hours, remove the cheese from the mold, unwrap, tip, and redress.

g) Make 3 quarts of saturated brine and chill to 50°F to 55°F. Remove the cheese from the mold and cloth and place in the brine to soak at 50°F to 55°F for 8 hours, tipping at least once during the brining process.

h) Remove the cheese from the brine and pat dry. Air-dry at room temperature on a cheese mat for 24 hours, or until the surface is dry to the touch. Place on a mat in a ripening box to age at 50°F and 90 percent humidity, Tipping every other day.

i) Before you tip the cheese the first time, make a brine wash: boil $\frac{1}{2}$ cup of water and let it cool, then add 1 teaspoon of kosher salt and stir to dissolve. Store in the refrigerator. Each time you tip the cheese, wipe the surface with a small piece of cheesecloth dipped in a small amount of brine wash.

j) The brine wash will control unwanted mold growth. Discard any unused brine wash and make a fresh batch each week. Also wipe away any moisture from the bottom, sides, and lid of the ripening box each time you tip the cheese.

k) Flip and wash the cheese every 2 days for 4 to 5 weeks. At 10 to 14 days, a light yellow-orange color will develop, deepening as the cheese ages. At 4 to 5 weeks, the rind should be moist but not sticky and the center of the cheese should feel soft. Consume within 2 weeks of desired ripeness.

BLUE CHEESES

93. Bloomy Blue Log Chèvre

MAKES Two 6-ounce logs

Ingredients

- 1 gallon pasteurized goat's milk
- 1 teaspoon Aroma B powdered mesophilic starter culture
- $\frac{1}{8}$ teaspoon Penicillium candidum mold powder
- Pinch of Geotrichum candidum 15 mold powder
- Pinch of Penicillium roqueforti mold powder
- 1 teaspoon calcium chloride diluted in $\frac{1}{4}$ cup cool nonchlorinated water
- 1 teaspoon liquid rennet diluted in $\frac{1}{4}$ cup cool nonchlorinated water
- 1 tablespoon sea salt
- $1\frac{1}{2}$ tablespoons vegetable ash

Directions

a) Heat the milk in a nonreactive 6-quart stockpot over low heat to 72°F; this should take 10 minutes. Turn off the heat.

b) Sprinkle the starter and mold powders over the milk and let rehydrate for 5 minutes. Mix well using a whisk in an up-and-down motion. Add the calcium chloride and gently whisk in for 1 minute, then add the rennet in the same way.

c) Cover and let sit, maintaining 72°F for 18 hours, or until the curds form a firm mass and the whey is coating on the top.

d) Place 2 Camembert or other round, straight-sided molds on a mat on a draining rack over a tray, and steady 2 cylindrical Saint-Maure molds inside them.

e) With a ladle or skimmer, gently cut $\frac{1}{2}$-inch-thick slices of curds and layer them in the cylindrical molds. Let drain until more curds can be added to the molds. Do not be tempted to add another mold; the curds will compress as the whey drains out, making room for all of the curds.

f) Cover the molds, rack, and tray with a kitchen towel and let the cheeses drain for 24 hours at room temperature.

Remove any accumulated whey a few times while draining, wiping out the tray when you do so. Flip the cheeses after 6 hours, or when they are firm enough to handle, then Dip them a few more times during the 24 hours. At the end of 24 hours, the curds will have reduced to about half the height of the molds.

g) Once the cheeses have stopped draining and the curds have compressed to below the halfway point of the molds, remove the molds and sprinkle 2 teaspoons of the salt over the entire surface of each cheese. Set on the rack for 10 minutes to allow the salt to dissolve.

h) In a small bowl or jar, combine the vegetable ash with the remaining 1 teaspoon of salt. Wearing disposable gloves, use a fine-mesh strainer to lightly dust the cheeses with vegetable ash, coating them completely. Gently pat the ash onto the surface of the cheeses.

i) Place the dusted cheeses at least 1 inch apart on a clean cheese mat in a ripening box. Cover the box loosely with the lid and let stand at room temperature for 24 hours. Let drain and wipe out any moisture from the box, then ripen the cheese at 50°F to 55°F and 90 percent humidity for 2 weeks.

j) For the first few days, adjust the lid to be slightly open for a portion of each day to maintain the desired humidity level. The surface of the cheese should appear moist but not wet.

k) Flip the cheeses one-quarter turn daily to maintain their log shape. After about 5 days, the first signs of white fuzzy mold will appear. After 10 to 14 days, the cheeses will be fully coated in white mold.

l) After 3 weeks, some of the dark ash will appear through the white mold. Left a bit longer, more dark ash will appear. After a total of 4 weeks from the start of ripening, wrap in cheese paper and store in the refrigerator. It is best to consume this cheese when it reaches your desired ripeness.

94.   Blue gouda

MAKES 1½ pounds

Ingredients

- 2 gallons pasteurized whole cow's milk
- 1 teaspoon Meso II powdered mesophilic starter culture ⅛ teaspoon Penicillium roqueforti mold powder
- 1 teaspoon calcium chloride diluted in ¼ cup cool nonchlorinated water (omit if using raw milk)
- 1 teaspoon liquid rennet diluted in ¼ cup cool nonchlorinated water
- Kosher salt or cheese salt

Directions

a) In a nonreactive 10-quart stockpot, heat the milk over low heat to 86°F; this should take 15 to 18 minutes. Turn off the heat.

b) Sprinkle the starter and mold powder over the milk and let rehydrate for 5 minutes. Mix in well using a whisk in an up-and-down motion. Cover and maintain 86°F, allowing the milk to ripen for 45 minutes. Add the calcium chloride and gently whisk in for 1 minute, then add the rennet in the same way.

c) Cover and let sit, maintaining 86°F for 30 minutes, or until the curds give a clean break.

d) Still maintaining 86°F, cut the curds into $\frac{1}{2}$-inch pieces and let sit for 5 minutes. Then stir for 5 minutes and let stand for 5 minutes. Heat 2 quarts of water to 140°F and maintain that heat. When the curds sink to the bottom of the pot, ladle 2 cups of the whey, then add enough 140°F water to bring the curds to 92°F.

e) Gently stir for 10 minutes, then let the curds settle. Ladle o enough whey to expose the tops of the curds, then add enough 140°F water to bring the curds to 98°F. Gently stir for 20 minutes, or until the curds have shrunk to the size of small beans. Let the curds settle for 10 minutes; they will knit together in the bottom of the pot.

f) Warm a colander with hot water, then drain the whey and place the knitted curds in the colander. Let drain for 5 minutes. Line a 5-inch tomme mold with damp cheesecloth and set it on a draining rack over a tray. Using your hands, break o 1-inch chunks of curd and distribute into the mold. Lightly press them into place to fill the gaps.

g) Pull the cloth up tight and smooth, cover the curds with the cloth tails and the follower, and press at 5 pounds for 30 minutes.

h) Remove the cheese from the mold, unwrap, tip, and redress, then press at 10 pounds for 6 hours.

i) Make 3 quarts of saturated brine and chill to 50°F to 55°F. Remove the cheese from the mold and cloth and place it in the brine to soak at 50°F to 55°F for 8 hours, tipping it once during the brining.

j) Remove the cheese from the brine and pat dry. Place on a rack and air-dry at room temperature for 1 to 2 days, or until the surface is dry to the touch.

k) Place on a mat in a ripening box, cover loosely, and age at 50°F to 55°F and 85 percent humidity for 1 week, Ripping daily. Remove any unwanted mold with a small piece of cheesecloth dampened in a vinegar-salt solution.

l) Coat with wax and store at 50°F to 55°F and 75 percent humidity for at least 6 weeks and up to 4 months. The cheese will be ready to eat at 6 weeks.

95.   Buttermilk blue

MAKES 10 ounces

Ingredients

- 2 quarts pasteurized whole cow's milk
- 1 quart cultured buttermilk, homemade (see variation on Crème Fraîche) or store-bought
- 2 cups heavy cream
- 1 teaspoon MM 100 powdered mesophilic starter culture Penicillium roqueforti mold powder
- 1 teaspoon calcium chloride diluted in $\frac{1}{4}$ cup cool nonchlorinated water
- 1 teaspoon liquid rennet diluted in $\frac{1}{4}$ cup cool nonchlorinated water
- $1\frac{1}{2}$ teaspoons kosher salt

Directions

a) In a 6-quart stockpot over low heat, heat the milk, buttermilk, and cream to 90°F; this should take about 20 minutes. Turn off the heat.

b) Sprinkle the starter and a pinch of the mold powder over the milk and let rehydrate for 5 minutes. Mix in well using a whisk in an up-and-down motion. Cover and maintain 90°F, allowing the milk to ripen for 30 minutes. Add the calcium chloride and gently whisk in, then add the rennet in the same way. Cover and maintain 90°F for $1\frac{1}{2}$ hours, or until the curds give a clean break.

c) Still maintaining 90°F, cut the curds into 1-inch pieces and let sit for 10 minutes. Then gently stir for 10 minutes to shrink the curds slightly and firm them up. Let stand for another 15 minutes, or until the curds sink to the bottom. Ladle o enough whey to expose the curds.

d) Line a colander with damp butter muslin and gently ladle the curds into it. Let drain for 10 minutes. Tie the corners of the cloth together to form a draining sack and hang for 20 minutes, or until the whey stops draining.

e) Line a 4-inch Camembert mold with damp butter muslin and place it on a rack over a tray. Gently ladle the curds into the mold, filling it to one-fourth its height and pressing down slightly with your hand to fill the gaps.

f) Measure out $\frac{1}{8}$ teaspoon of P. roqueforti powder. Lightly sprinkle the curds with one-third of the mold powder, then add more curds to fill the mold halfway, again gently pressing to fill the gaps and sprinkling another one-third of the mold powder over the curds.

g) Repeat to fill the mold with two more layers of curds and one of mold powder; the curds should come up to about 1 inch from the top of the mold. Pull the cloth up tight and smooth and cover the curds with the cloth tails. Let the cheese drain for 4 hours at room temperature, then unwrap, Dip, redress, and let drain for 4 more hours.

h) Carefully remove the cheese from the mold, unwrap, and sprinkle one side with $\frac{3}{4}$ teaspoon of the salt. Flip the cheese and place the cheese mold over it. The cheese will be fairly fragile, so handle it gently. Place it on a mat in a ripening box and sprinkle the remaining $\frac{3}{4}$ teaspoon of salt on the top.

i) Let drain for 5 hours, then remove the mold. Dry salt the sides of the cheese. Put the cheese in a ripening box, cover loosely with the lid, and age at 54°F and 75 percent humidity for up to 1 week, or until the whey stops draining.

j) Flip the cheese daily, draining o any whey that may have accumulated in the ripening box and using a paper towel to wipe any moisture from the bottom, sides, and lid of the box.

k) Once the whey has stopped draining, use a sterilized knitting needle or round skewer to pierce the cheese all the way through to the other side, four times horizontally and four times vertically. These air passages will encourage mold growth.

l) Secure the lid of the ripening box and ripen at 50°F and 85 to 90 percent humidity. Blue mold should appear on the exterior after 10 days. Watch the cheese carefully, tipping it daily and adjusting the lid if the humidity increases and too much moisture develops.

m) Over the next 2 weeks, pierce the cheese one or two more times in the same locations to ensure proper aeration and blue vein development. If any excessive or undesirable mold appears on the exterior of the cheese, rub it o with a small piece of cheesecloth dipped in a vinegar-salt solution.

n) Ripen for 6 weeks, rub o any excess mold with dry cheesecloth, then wrap the cheese in foil and store refrigerated for up to 3 more months or longer for a more pronounced flavor.

96. Cambozola

MAKES Two 10-ounce cheeses

Ingredients

- 2 gallon pasteurized whole cow's milk
- 2 gallon pasteurized heavy cream
- 1 teaspoon Meso II or C101 powdered mesophilic starter culture
- $\frac{1}{8}$ teaspoon Penicillium candidum mold powder
- 1 teaspoon calcium chloride diluted in $\frac{1}{4}$ cup cool nonchlorinated water
- 1 teaspoon liquid rennet diluted in $\frac{1}{4}$ cup cool nonchlorinated water
- $\frac{1}{8}$ teaspoon Penicillium roqueforti mold powder
- 4 teaspoons kosher salt

Directions

a) Combine the milk and cream in a nonreactive 6-quart stockpot set in a 96°F water bath over low heat and gently warm to 86°F; this should take about 10 minutes. Turn off the heat.

b) Sprinkle the starter and P. candidum mold powder over the milk and let rehydrate for 5 minutes. Mix in well using a whisk in an up-and-down motion. Cover and maintain 86°F, allowing the milk to ripen for 30 minutes. Add the calcium chloride and gently whisk in, then add the rennet in the same way. Cover and let sit, maintaining 86°F for $1\frac{1}{2}$ hours, or until the curds give a clean break.

c) Cut the curds into $\frac{1}{2}$-inch pieces and gently stir for 5 minutes. Let the curds rest for 5 minutes.

d) Line a colander with damp cheesecloth and gently ladle the curds into it. Let drain for minutes.

e) Line 2 Saint-Maure molds with damp cheesecloth and set them on a draining rack over a tray. Using a skimmer, gently ladle the curds into the molds until half full. Sprinkle the top of each cheese with half of the P. roqueforti mold powder, then top each mold with the remaining curds. Let drain for 6 hours at room temperature, draining o and wiping out any whey that collects.

f) Remove any accumulated whey a few times during draining, wiping out the tray when you do so. When the cheeses are firm enough to handle (after about 8 hours), unmold and unwrap them and discard the cheesecloth, then Hip them and return them to the unlined molds. Unmold and Lip one more time while the cheeses are draining. The cheeses should drain for 8 to 10 hours total.

g) Once the cheeses have stopped draining, remove them from the molds and place on a clean mat set in a clean, dry ripening box. Sprinkle 2 teaspoons of the salt over the tops of the cheeses and wait 5 minutes for the salt to dissolve. Flip the cheeses over and sprinkle the tops with the remaining 2 teaspoons of salt.

h) Cover the box loosely with its lid. Ripen at 50°F to 55°F and 90 percent humidity. High humidity is essential for making this cheese. Flip the cheeses daily, wiping away any whey that accumulates in the ripening box. When the cheeses are dry on the surface (after about 3 days), cover the box tightly to continue ripening.

i) Continue to tip the cheeses daily and remove any moisture in the box. After about 5 days, the first signs of white fuzzy mold will appear. When the cheeses are fully coated in white mold (after about 8 days), aerate the center of each cheese by piercing horizontally from the sides through the center to the other side using a sterilized knitting needle or skewer.

j) There should be 8 to 10 piercings through each cheese to allow proper development of blue veins. Pierce again in the same places if any holes close up over the next 10 to 12 days.

k) Wrap in cheese paper 10 to 12 days after piercing and return to the ripening box. The cheese will begin to soften within 1 week or so.

l) After a total of 4 weeks from the start
    of ripening, the cheese should be ready
    to eat, or continue to ripen to 6 weeks in
    the refrigerator.

97. Coastal blue

MAKES Two 1-pound cheeses

Ingredients

- 2 gallons pasteurized whole cow's milk
- 1 teaspoon MM 100 powdered mesophilic starter culture
- $\frac{1}{8}$ teaspoon Penicillium roqueforti mold powder
- $\frac{1}{4}$ teaspoon calcium chloride diluted in $\frac{1}{4}$ cup cool nonchlorinated water
- $\frac{1}{4}$ teaspoon liquid rennet diluted in $\frac{1}{4}$ cup cool nonchlorinated water
- 2 tablespoons coarse kosher salt

Directions

a) In a nonreactive 10-quart stockpot set in a 96°F water bath over low heat, gently warm the milk to 86°F; this should take about 10 minutes. Turn off the heat.

b) Sprinkle the starter and the mold powder over the milk and let rehydrate for 5 minutes. Mix well using a whisk in an up-and-down motion. Cover and maintain 86°F, letting the milk ripen for 1 hour, stirring every once in a while.

Add the calcium chloride and gently whisk in, then add the rennet in the same way. Cover and let sit, maintaining 86°F for 1 to 1½ hours, or until the curds give a clean break.

c) Cut the curds into ½-inch pieces and gently stir for 10 minutes, then let the curds settle to the bottom of the pot. Ladle out 2 quarts of whey and stir the curds for 5 more minutes.

d) Line a colander or strainer with damp butter muslin and gently ladle the curds into it. Let drain for 5 minutes. Line two 4-inch Camembert molds with damp cheesecloth and set them on a draining rack over a tray.

e) Ladle the curds into the molds, pull the cloth up around the curds and cover the top with the tails of the cloth, and let drain for 12 hours at room temperature. Flip the cheeses at least four times to ensure a uniform shape and appearance.

f) Remove the cheeses from the molds and sprinkle 1 tablespoon of salt over the entire surface of each, coating them evenly. Gently pat the salt into the surface. Set the cheeses on a mat in a ripening box and age at 68°F to 72°F and 90 percent humidity. Set the lid ajar a little so there is some air movement. Flip the cheeses daily, wiping away any excess moisture from the box with a paper towel.

g) After 2 days, use a sterilized knitting needle or round skewer to pierce each cheese all the way through to the other side, 4 times horizontally and 4 times vertically. These air passages will encourage mold growth.

h) Place the cheeses back in the box and ripen at 50°F to 56°F and 85 percent humidity for 3 to 4 weeks. After 10 days, blue mold should start to appear. Flip the cheeses daily, wiping away any excess moisture from the box with a paper towel. Rub o any undesirable mold with a piece of cheesecloth dipped in a vinegar-salt solution and wrung to dry.

i) After sufficient blue mold growth is achieved, wrap them in tightly in foil and refrigerate for up to 4 to 6 months.

98. Gorgonzola

MAKES 1½ pounds

Ingredients

- 6 quarts pasteurized whole cow's milk
- 1 teaspoon MM 100 powdered mesophilic starter culture
- 1 teaspoon calcium chloride diluted in ¼ cup cool nonchlorinated water
- ½ teaspoon liquid rennet diluted in ¼ cup cool nonchlorinated water
- ⅛ teaspoon Penicillium roqueforti mold powder
- Kosher salt

Directions

a) In a nonreactive 4-quart stockpot set in a 100°F water bath, gently warm 3 quarts of the milk to 90°F; this should take about 15 minutes. Turn off the heat.

b) Sprinkle half of the starter over the milk and let it rehydrate for 5 minutes. Mix in well using a whisk in an up-and-down motion. Cover and maintain 90°F, letting the milk ripen for 30 minutes. Add half of the calcium chloride and gently whisk in, then add half of the rennet in the same way. Cover and let sit, maintaining 90°F for 30 minutes, or until the curds give a clean break.

c) Cut the curds into ¾-inch pieces and let rest for 10 minutes, then gently stir for 20 minutes to firm up the curds slightly. Let rest for another 15 minutes, or until the curds sink to the bottom.

d) Ladle out enough whey to expose the curds. Line a colander with damp cheesecloth and gently ladle the curds into it. Let drain for 5 minutes. Tie the corners of the cheesecloth together to form a draining sack and hang at 55°F to let drain for 8 hours or overnight.

e) The next morning, make a second batch of curds in the same manner, using the other half of the milk, starter, calcium chloride, and rennet. Let the curds drain at 55°F for 6 hours. Before the second batch is done draining, bring the first batch to room temperature.

f) Untie the sacks and, keeping the batches separate, break the curds into 1-inch chunks. Line a 4-inch Camembert mold with damp cheesecloth and place it on a draining rack.

g) Using your hands, line the bottom and sides of the mold with a thin layer of the second batch of curds. Press down slightly to Fill the gaps.

h) Layer half of the curds from the first batch in the mold and gently press down to fill the gaps.

i) Sprinkle the top with one-third of the P. roqueforti mold powder, then repeat the process two more times until the mold is Filled with four layers of curds, alternating first-batch and second-batch curds and Finishing with second-batch curds. The mold should be Filled to about 1 inch from the top.

j) Pull the cheesecloth up around the curds and cover the top with the tails of the cloth and the follower. Press at 5 pounds for 2 hours, then unmold, unwrap, tip, and redress.

k) Press at 8 pounds for 2 hours. Press at 8 pounds for 6 more hours, unwrapping, tipping, and redressing every 2 hours.

l) Carefully remove the cheese from the mold, unwrap, and sprinkle one side with $\frac{3}{4}$ teaspoon of salt. tip the cheese over and place the cheese mold over it. The cheese will be fairly fragile, so handle it gently. Place it on a mat in a ripening box and sprinkle $\frac{3}{4}$ teaspoon of salt over the top. Let drain for 5 hours, then tip the cheese again. Repeat this process once a day for 3 more days, sprinkling a pinch of salt on each side the first time you tip it each day, then draining for 5 hours and tipping once again. Each time you Rip the cheese, drain any accumulated whey and wipe the box dry with a paper towel.

m) After the 4 days of salting, Dipping, and draining, remove the mold and cover the ripening box loosely with the lid. Age at 50°F and 75 percent humidity for up to 2 weeks, or until the whey stops draining. Flip the cheese daily, removing any whey that accumulates in the ripening box and wiping any moisture from the sides of the box.

n) Once the whey has stopped draining, use a sterilized knitting needle or round skewer to pierce the cheese all the way through to the other side, 4 times horizontally and 4 times vertically. These air passages will encourage mold growth.

o) Secure the lid of the ripening box and ripen at 50°F and 85 to 90 percent humidity. Blue mold should appear on the exterior after 10 days. Watch the cheese carefully, turning it daily and adjusting the lid if the humidity increases and too much moisture develops. Remove any unwanted mold with a piece of cheesecloth dipped in a vinegar-salt solution.

p) Over the 2 weeks after the initial piercing, pierce the cheese one or two more times in the same locations to ensure proper aeration and blue vein development.

q) Ripen for 2 months, then wrap the cheese in foil and store refrigerated for 1 to 3 more months.

99. Roquefort

MAKES 1 pound

Ingredients

- 2 quarts pasteurized whole cow's milk
- 2 quarts heavy cream
- 1 teaspoon MA 4001 powdered mesophilic starter culture
- 1 teaspoon mild lipase powder diluted in $\frac{1}{4}$ cup cool nonchlorinated water 20 minutes before using
- 1 teaspoon calcium chloride diluted in $\frac{1}{4}$ cup cool nonchlorinated water (omit if using raw milk)
- 1 teaspoon liquid rennet diluted in $\frac{1}{4}$ cup cool nonchlorinated water
- $\frac{1}{8}$ teaspoon Penicillium roqueforti mold powder
- $1\frac{1}{2}$ teaspoons kosher salt

Directions

a) In a nonreactive 6-quart stockpot set in a 100°F water bath, combine the milk and cream and gently warm to 90°F; this should take about 15 minutes. Turn off the heat.

b) Sprinkle the starter over the milk and let rehydrate for 5 minutes. Mix well using a whisk in an up-and-down motion. Cover and maintain 90°F, allowing the milk to ripen for few minutes. Add the lipase, if using, and gently whisk in, then gently whisk in the calcium chloride and then the rennet. Cover and let sit, maintaining 90°F for 2 hours, or until the curds give a clean break.

c) Cut the curds into 1-inch pieces and let rest for 15 minutes, then gently stir to firm up the curds slightly. Let rest for another 15 minutes, or until the curds sink to the bottom.

d) Ladle out enough whey to expose the curds. Line a colander with damp cheesecloth and gently ladle the curds into it. Let drain for 10 minutes. Tie the corners of the cheesecloth together to form a draining sack and hang at room temperature to let drain for 30 minutes, or until the whey stops dripping.

e) Set a 4-inch Camembert mold on a draining rack and line it with damp cheesecloth. Using your hands, layer one-fourth of the curds into the mold. Gently press down to fill in the gaps.

f) Sprinkle the top of the curds with one-third of the P. roqueforti mold powder, then repeat the process until the mold is filled, finishing with a layer of curds. The mold should be filled to about 1 inch from the top.

g) Let drain at room temperature for 8 hours. Once the curds have firmed enough to handle, after about 4 hours of draining, tip the cheese a time or two, keeping it in its cheesecloth. After 8 hours, remove the cheese from the mold, unwrap, tip, and redress, then let drain for 16 hours at room temperature.

h) After 24 hours of draining, carefully remove the cheese from the mold, sprinkle one side with $\frac{3}{4}$ teaspoon of the salt, then tip it over and place it on a mat in a ripening box.

i) Sprinkle the remaining $\frac{3}{4}$ teaspoon of salt over the top. The cheese will be fairly fragile at this point, so handle it gently.

j) Cover the box loosely and ripen the cheese at 50°F to 55°F and 85 to 90 percent humidity. Flip the cheese daily for 1 week, draining any accumulated liquid in the ripening box and using a paper towel to wipe any moisture from the box.

k) After 1 week, use a sterilized knitting needle or round skewer to pierce the cheese all the way through to the other side 4 times horizontally and 4 times vertically.

l) These passages will encourage mold growth. Continue to ripen at 50°F to 55°F and 85 to 90 percent humidity. Blue mold should appear on the exterior after 10 days.

m) Once the cheese has stopped draining whey, secure the box's lid to control the humidity. Flip the cheese daily and adjust the lid if the humidity increases and too much moisture develops.

n) Over the 2 weeks after the piercing, pierce one or two more times in the same locations to ensure proper aeration and blue vein development. Remove any excessive or unwanted mold with a piece of cheesecloth dipped in a vinegar-salt solution.

o) Ripen the cheese for 6 to 8 weeks. When it reaches the desired creamy texture, wrap it in foil and store it, refrigerated, for up to 4 more months.

100. Stilton

MAKES 1 pound

Ingredients

- 1 gallon pasteurized whole cow's milk
- 1 cup heavy cream
- Penicillium roqueforti mold powder
- 1 teaspoon C101 or Meso II powdered mesophilic starter culture
- 1 teaspoon calcium chloride diluted in $\frac{1}{4}$ cup cool nonchlorinated water
- 1 teaspoon liquid rennet diluted in $\frac{1}{4}$ cup cool nonchlorinated water
- 4 teaspoons kosher salt

Directions

a) In a nonreactive 6-quart stockpot, heat the milk and cream over low heat to 86°F; this should take about 15 minutes. Turn off the heat.

b) Sprinkle $\frac{1}{8}$ teaspoon of the mold powder and the starter over the milk and let rehydrate for 5 minutes. Mix well using a whisk in an up-and-down motion. Cover and maintain 86°F, allowing the milk to ripen for 30 minutes. Add the calcium chloride and gently whisk in, then add the rennet in the same way.

c) Cover and let sit, maintaining 86°F for $1\frac{1}{2}$ hours, or until the curds give a clean break.

d) Using a skimmer, slice the curds into $\frac{1}{2}$-inch-thick slabs. Line a colander with damp cheesecloth and set it over a bowl about the same size as the colander.

e) Transfer the curd slices to the colander; the curds should be sitting in the whey caught in the bowl. Cover the colander, maintain 86°F for $1\frac{1}{2}$ hours. Then tie the corners of the cheesecloth together to form a draining sack and hang to let drain at room temperature for 30 minutes, or until the whey stops dripping.

f) Set the sack on a cutting board, open the cheesecloth, and gently press down on the curds, forming them into a brick shape. Redress the curds in the same cheesecloth and place on a draining rack. Press them at 8 pounds for 8 hours or overnight at room temperature.

g) Remove the curds from the cheesecloth and break them into approximately 1-inch pieces. Place the curds in a bowl, add the salt, and gently toss to combine.

h) Line a 4½-inch-diameter round cheese mold with damp cheesecloth and set it on a draining rack. Layer half of the curds into the mold. Sprinkle the top with a pinch of P. roqueforti mold powder, then layer the remaining curds in the mold.

i) Fold the tails of the cloth over the curds, set the follower in place, and let drain at room temperature for 4 days. Flip every 20 minutes for the first 2 hours, every 2 hours for the next 6 hours, and once a day for the next 4 days. Remove any accumulated whey each time you tip the cheese.

j) After the 4 days of draining, remove the cheese from the mold and cloth and place it on a clean mat in a dry ripening box. Cover the box loosely with the lid and ripen the cheese at 50°F to 55°F and 85 to 90 percent humidity. High humidity is essential for making this cheese.

k) Flip the cheese daily for 1 week, removing any whey that accumulates in the ripening box and wiping any moisture from the box. Wipe the rind daily with cheesecloth soaked in a simple brine solution for the first week.

l) When the cheese is dry on the surface, secure the lid of the ripening box tightly and continue to ripen at 50°F to 55°F and 90 percent humidity, tipping once or twice a week.

m) After 2 weeks, the cheese should have developed a slightly moldy exterior. At 4 months, wrap the cheese in foil and store refrigerated for up to 2 more months.

CONCLUSION

Cheese is a good source of calcium, a key nutrient for healthy bones and teeth, blood clotting, wound healing, and maintaining normal blood pressure. ... One ounce of cheddar cheese provides 20 percent of this daily requirement. However, cheese can also be high in calories, sodium, and saturated fat. Cheese is delicious as well!!

When made properly, homemade cheese is often times better for you than store bought or commercial cheeses because they don't contain as much preservatives or other harmful, artificial ingredients. So what are you waiting for?

CPSIA information can be obtained
at www.ICGtesting.com
Printed in the USA
LVHW080545200522
719277LV00002B/14